MYSTAT
STATISTICAL APPLICATIONS

MACINTOSH EDITION

Robert L. Hale
■ The Pennsylvania State University ■

Course Technology, Inc.
One Main Street
Cambridge, MA 02142

MYSTAT: Statistical Applications, Macintosh Edition is published by Course Technology, Inc.

Product Management	Katherine T. Pinard
	David Crocco
Production Management	Josh Bernoff
Text Design/DesktopPublishing	Debbie Crane
Cover Design	Darci Mehall
Quality Assurance	Mark Valentine
	Rob Spadoni
	Melissa Heiger
	Liz Chung
Index	Cornelia Robart
Manufacturing	Mark Dec

MYSTAT: Statistical Applications, Macintosh Edition © 1992 Course Technology, Inc. Portions © 1990 SYSTAT, Inc. used by permission.

All rights reserved. Printed in the U.S.A. This publication is protected by federal copyright law. No part of this publication may be reproduced, stored in a retrieval system, or transmitted in any form or by any means, electronic, mechanical, photocopying, recording, or otherwise, or be used to make any derivative work (such as translation or adaptation) without prior permission in writing from Course Technology, Inc.

Trademarks

Course Technology and the open book logo are trademarks of Course Technology, Inc.

MYSTAT and SYSTAT are registered trademarks of SYSTAT, Inc.

Some of the product names used in this book have been used for identification purposes only and may be trademarks or registered trademarks of their respective manufacturers and sellers.

Disclaimer

Course Technology, Inc. reserves the right to revise this publication and make changes from time to time in its content without notice.

ISBN 1-878748-62-9

Preface

When I first began learning statistics, the only substantial calculation tool available was the slide-rule. Because every slide-rule performed the same functions in the same manner and the simple mathematical operations could be taught in a few hours, statistics instructors consciously integrated this calculation instrument into class.

Next came the electronic calculator. Its operation was much easier than the slide-rule. Formerly tedious calculations were performed almost instantaneously. Calculators were swiftly adopted by statistics instructors and students and were integrated into both classroom lectures and textbooks.

The calculator and slide-rule only helped to solve the computation problems; they did little to help reveal the deeper meanings of statistical decision theory. Students had to understand the calculation formulas in order to be successful with the tool. Many students felt an overwhelming amount of time was devoted to the mathematics, and far too little time was spent on the assumptions and theoretical issues behind the statistical procedures. Often students could perform calculations on examinations, but they couldn't explain why one statistical procedure was used instead of another. Statistics class was often dreaded because of the math, and all excitement about the power that statistics provides to help make important research decisions for human welfare or business was lost.

With the proliferation of personal computers and statistical software programs, the learning scene has changed for the better. With current tools—a personal computer and a user-friendly statistics package—it is possible to answer statistical questions without spending inordinate amounts of time calculating the solution. To teach students how to do this successfully, however, it is necessary to integrate today's tools thoroughly into the classroom. With this integration, statistics instructors can concentrate on teaching the assumptions and theoretical issues of statistics, instead of teaching basic mathematical calculations. The tutorials and examples in this text enable the computer to become more than a simple computation tool; it can be a learning tool.

Content and Organization

MYSTAT: Statistical Applications is coordinated with the learning sequence presented in the typical introductory statistics text. With only a few exceptions, (for example, where there is a reference to data or an illustration presented in a previous chapter) the chapters are independent, and can be taught in any order.

Chapter 1   explains how to install MYSTAT, then briefly describes the MYSTAT Data Editor.

Chapter 2   introduces the students to data entry. Students learn how to enter and save data, how to create new variables, how to find specific cases using an *If...then* expression, and how read a text file with MYSTAT.

Chapters 3 and **4**   give an introduction to descriptive statistics using MYSTAT to graph single variables and to calculate descriptive statistics.

Chapter 5 shows how to use MYSTAT to calculate one-sample z- and t-tests. Although MYSTAT can not directly calculate one-sample tests, the chapter shows how to use the software to do these calculations. MYSTAT's ZIF function, used to find the probability given the z-value, and ZCF function, used to find the z-value given the probability, are also described. Although the paired t-test is used in one-sample situations, initial discussion of this procedure is not presented until chapter 6 (*Two-Sample Statistical Tests*), because the procedure is more involved than the single sample examples presented in this chapter.

Chapter 6 uses MYSTAT to calculate t-tests for both one- and two-sample situations.

Chapter 7 explains how to use MYSTAT to calculate ANOVA.

Chapter 8 gives an introduction to graphs. Proper graphic design is explained and students learn how to construct scatterplots.

Chapter 9 describes correlation and regression techniques.

Chapter 10 gives the students an introduction to ANCOVA and explains how to use MYSTAT's ANOVA function to calculate ANCOVA statistics.

Chapter 11 explains how to use MYSTAT to calculate non-parametric statistics.

Pedagogical Features

Six-Step Solution

The six-step solution appears in each chapter that discusses a statistical test. The six steps provide a consistent framework for students to use to find a solution to a given problem. The steps guide the student through constructing the null and alternative hypotheses, setting the probability, calculating the stastistic using MYSTAT, and interpreting and analyzing the results.

Decision Charts

Each chapter that introduces a statistical test includes decision charts. These charts are designed to help students decide which statistical test is required for the data and problem being studied.

Data Disk

In addition to the MYSTAT software, *MYSTAT: Statistical Applications* comes with a student data disk. All the data used in the text and in the exercises are provided on the disk. The students can spend their time studying the data instead of keying it in, and, because the data is already on disk, data entry errors are avoided.

End of Chapter Exercises

Exercises are provided at the end of each chapter. Some of the exercises use data that has been used in the chapter; other exercises use entirely new data. All are designed to give the students practice in using MYSTAT to describe and make decisions about data.

Acknowledgements

I would like to thank John Connolly, Kitty Pinard, and David Crocco from Course Technology for all their assistance. Without their vision of integrating technological advances into the college curriculum, this book would have been impossible. I would also like to thank Debbie Crane for her wonderful interior design and for implementing it so quickly. And finally, I would like to thank Melissa Heiger and Liz Chung for the many hours they spent working through chapter drafts making sure that the directions were clear, and the results both correct and understandable.

It is also a pleasure to articulate my appreciation to the following reviewers for their thoughtful comments: Tony Dubitsky, ASI Market Research, Inc.; Lawrence Gall, Yale University; Rebecca German, University of Cincinnati; and C. Lincoln Johnson, University of Notre Dame.

Thanks also go to Leland Wilkinson, Mary Ann Hill, and Eve Goldman of SYSTAT, Inc. for their suggestions as the text was being developed.

Finally, I would like to thank my wife, my son, and my mother for all their support through the years. Without their encouragement and my father's many days of working overtime to sustain my undergraduate studies, I would not have been able to obtain any of my goals. Thanks, Dad!

From the Publisher...

At Course Technology, Inc. we are very excited about bringing you, college professors and students, the most practical and affordable technology-related products available.

The Course Technology Development Process

Our development process is unparalleled in the higher education publishing industry. Every product we create goes through an exacting process of design, development, review, and testing.

Reviewers give us direction and insight that shape our manuscripts and bring them up to the latest standards. Every manuscript is quality tested. Students whose background matches the intended audience work through every keystroke, carefully checking for clarity, and pointing out errors in logic and sequence. Together with our own technical reviewers, these testers help us to ensure that everything which carries our name is error-free and easy to use.

Course Technology Products

We show both **how** and **why** technology is critical to solving problems in college and in whatever field you choose to teach or pursue. Our time-tested, step-by-step instructions provide unparalleled clarity. Examples and applications are chosen and crafted to motivate students.

The Course Technology Team

This book will suit your needs because it was delivered quickly, efficiently and affordably. In every aspect of our business, we rely on a commitment to quality and the use of technology. Every employee contributes. The names of all of our employees, each equity holders in the company, are listed below:

Stephen M. Bayle, Josh Bernoff, Jan Boni, Irene Brennan, Susan Collins, John M. Connolly, Rebecca Costello, Debbie Crane, David Crocco, Mark Dec, Yvette Delgado, Katie Donovan, Joseph B. Dougherty, Susan Feinberg, Lori Glass, Suzanne Goguen, David Haar, Deanne Hart, Nicole Jones, Matt Kenslea, Peter Lester, Laurie Michelangelo, Kim Munsell, Paul Murphy, Amy Oliver, Debbie Parlee, George J. Pilla, Katherine Pinard, Diana Simeon, Robert Spadoni, Kathy Sutherland, Mark Valentine

Brief Contents

1	MYSTAT Overview	1
2	Data Editor	13
3	Graphing Data (Single Variables)	39
4	Descriptive Statistics	59
5	One-Sample Statistical Tests	69
6	Two-Sample Statistical Tests	85
7	Analysis of Variance	97
8	Graphing Data—Two or More Variables	109
9	Correlation and Regression	135
10	An Introduction to Analysis of Covariance	155
11	Nonparametric Statistical Tests	165

Contents

1 MYSTAT Overview — 1

Objectives 1

Installing MYSTAT 2
   Hard Disk Installation 2
   Floppy Disk Installation 5

MYSTAT Menu Bar 9
   File Menu 10
   Edit Menu 10
   Data Menu 10
   Graph Menu 10
   Analyze Menu 11
   Goodies Menu 11
   Editor Menu 11

MYSTAT Windows 11
   Data Editor Window 11
   View Window 11
   Commands Window 11
   Analysis Window 12

Obtaining Help 12

Quitting MYSTAT 12

2 Data Editor — 13

Objectives 13

The MYSTAT Data Editor 14

Keyboard Entry 15
   Naming Variables 16

Editing Data 18

Saving Data 19

Transforming Data 21
   Using the Math... Command 21
   Using the Recode... Command 23

Finding Specific Cases 26

Reading Text Files *28*

A Special Note on Printing Data Sets *31*

Odds and Ends *31*
  Functions, Relations, and Operators 31
  Filling the Worksheet 32
  The Sort, Rank, and Weight Commands 33
  Formatting Input 35
  Formatting Output 36
  Directing Your Results 37
  Using the Clipboard 37
  Exercises 38

3 Graphing Data (Single Variables) 39
  Objectives 39

What Are Graphs? *40*

Histograms *40*
  Producing and Printing Histograms 40

Stem-and-Leaf Graphs *44*

Box Plots *49*

Series Graphs *51*

Proper Graphic Design *54*
  Moving Graphs in the View Window 54
  Resizing Graphs 55

Saving Graphs as PICT Files *56*
  Exercises 56

4 Descriptive Statistics 59
  Objectives 59

Meanings of the Statistics *60*

Doing the Calculations *61*
  Using Redo Last Analysis 62

Calculating Statistics for Grouped Data *63*

Printing Data Sets *67*
  Exercises 68

5 One-Sample Statistical Tests — 69

Objectives 69

Determining Whether the One-sample z- or t-Test Is Appropriate *70*
  ZIF 72
  ZCF 73

One-Sample z-Test *75*

One-Sample t-Test *78*
  Exercises 83

6 Two-Sample Statistical Tests — 85

Objectives 85

Independent Versus Dependent t-test *86*

Independent t-Test *86*

Dependent t-Test *89*
  Two-Sample Situation 89
  One-Sample Situation 92
  Exercises 94

7 Analysis of Variance — 97

Objectives 97

One-Way ANOVA Versus Multi-Way ANOVA *98*

One-Way ANOVA *99*

Two-Way ANOVA *102*
  Exercises 105

8 Graphing Data—Two or More Variables — 109

Objectives 109

Two-Variable Scatterplots *110*
  Scatterplot Interpretation 111

Functional and Statistical Relationships *114*

Identifying Scatterplot Data Points *115*
  Scatterplot Brushing: Left Arrow 116
  Scatterplot Brushing: Flashlight 117
  The Flashlight and Multiple Data Points 118

Producing Scatterplots with Regression Lines *122*

Influence Plots *126*

Bubble Plots *127*

Other Plot Dialog Box Options *128*

Overlaying Graphs *129*
  Exercises 132

9 Correlation and Regression 135
Objectives 135

Determining Whether to Use Corr or Regress *136*

Correlation Coefficients *136*
  Pearson Product-Moment Correlation 137
  Calculation of r 137
  Spearman Rank 141
  Calculating r_s 142

Bivariate Regression Analysis *143*
  Assumptions for Regression Analysis 146

Multiple Regression Analysis *146*

Outlier Detection *149*
  Leverage 149
  Studentized Deleted Residuals 149
  Cook's D 150
  Exercises 152

10 An Introduction to Analysis of Covariance 155
Objectives 155

Determining Whether ANCOVA Is Appropriate *156*

What Is ANCOVA? *156*
  The ANOVA Solution 158

Assumptions of ANCOVA *162*
  Exercises 163

11 Nonparametric Statistical Tests 165

Objectives 165

Determining Which Nonparametric Procedure to Use *166*

One-way Chi-Square *167*

Two-way Chi-Square *171*

Other Measures of Association 173
Options in the Tables Dialog Box 174

Other Nonparametrics *175*

Sign Test *175*

The Wilcoxon Matched-Pairs Signed Ranks Test *178*

Friedman Two-way ANOVA *180*

Notched Box Plots *181*

Exercises 183

References *R-1*

1

MYSTAT Overview

MYSTAT is an interactive statistics and graphics package. With MYSTAT, users can compute most of the descriptive and inferential statistics typically covered in a two-semester college course. MYSTAT graphs aid in visualizing both one- and two-dimensional data. MYSTAT can be used on IBM PC-compatible and Macintosh computers and VAX/VMS systems. This text describes MYSTAT features on a Macintosh. To run on a Macintosh, MYSTAT requires one megabyte of memory and either a hard disk drive or two 800K floppy disk drives. MYSTAT can handle up to fifty variables and 32,000 cases.

Objectives

At the end of this tutorial you should be able to
- Install MYSTAT
- Start MYSTAT
- Understand MYSTAT's seven menus
- Understand the different windows used by MYSTAT
- Obtain MYSTAT's on-screen help
- Quit MYSTAT

■ Installing MYSTAT

This tutorial describes how to install MYSTAT. The MYTAT program and the data files that will be used in the tutorials and the exercises are contained on the disk that comes with this text. You must complete one of the installation procedures before you can run MYSTAT. You cannot run MYSTAT using the disk that comes with this text because there is not enough space on the disk. If you have a hard disk and one floppy drive, continue with the following section "Hard Disk Installation." If you have two floppy drives, skip to the section "Floppy Disk Installation" on page 5.

Hard Disk Installation

To install MYSTAT on a hard disk, you'll create a MYSTAT folder on the hard drive and copy the MYSTAT program files from the MYSTAT Program and Data disk that comes with this text into this folder.

To install MYSTAT on a hard disk,

1. Turn on your Macintosh. Once the system is running, you should see an icon that represents the hard disk.
2. Double-click on the hard disk icon to display its contents.
3. Select **New Folder** from the **File** menu. A new folder appears in the window displaying the contents of your hard drive.
4. Drag the cursor across the title of the folder to highlight it, then type **MYSTAT Program**.
5. Make sure the original MYSTAT Program and Data disk that comes with this text is locked, then insert it into the floppy disk drive.
6. Double click on the MYSTAT Program and Data disk icon. You will see a window like the one shown in Figure 1.1.

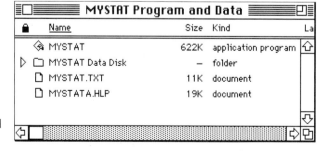

Figure 1.1
The contents of the MYSTAT Program and Data disk

7. Press and hold [**Shift**]. While holding [Shift] down, click on the files MYSTAT, MYSTAT.TXT, and MYSTATA.HLP. Let go of [**Shift**]. The three files should be highlighted in the window.

8. Drag the three files onto the MYSTAT Program folder icon. The files will be copied to the MYSTAT Program folder.

9. After the three files have been copied, double-click on the MYSTAT Program folder and make sure that all three files are in it. The MYSTAT Program folder window should look similar to Figure 1.2. Your screen may look different if an option other than **by Name** is checked in the **View** menu.

Figure 1.2
The contents of the MYSTAT Program folder

10. Click on the MYSTAT Program and Data disk window. If you are using System 6, select **Eject** from the **File** menu. If you are using System 7, select **Eject** from the **Special** menu. The disk will eject and its icon and the window will stay on the screen.

Now you need to copy the data files to a floppy disk.

1. Get an unitialized floppy disk and label it Data Disk.
2. Insert the Data Disk into the floppy disk drive. A dialog box like the one shown in Figure 1.3 will appear.

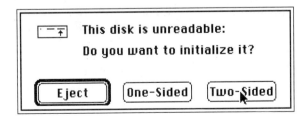

Figure 1.3
The disk initialization dialog box

3. Click **Two-Sided**. A message will appear warning you that this process will erase all information on the disk.
4. Click **Erase**.
5. The system now asks you to name this disk. Type **Data Disk**, and click **OK**. When the initialization is complete, the icon for this disk will appear on the screen.

6. Click on the Data Disk icon. If you are using System 6, select **Eject** from the **File** menu. If you are using System 7, select **Eject** from the **Special** menu. The disk will eject but the icon will stay on the screen.
7. Make sure the original MYSTAT Program and Data disk that comes with this book is locked, then insert it into the drive.
8. Double-click on the MYSTAT Data Disk folder icon in the MYSTAT Program and Data window.
9. Choose **Select All** from the **Edit** menu. All of the files in the MYSTAT Data folder will be highlighted.
10. Drag the files onto the Data Disk icon to copy them to the Data Disk.

    You may be prompted to switch disks while the files are being copied. Follow the instructions on the screen.
11. Double click on the Data Disk icon to make sure that the data files were copied. Your screen should look similar to Figure 1.4. Your screen may look different if an option other then **by Name** is checked in the **View** menu.

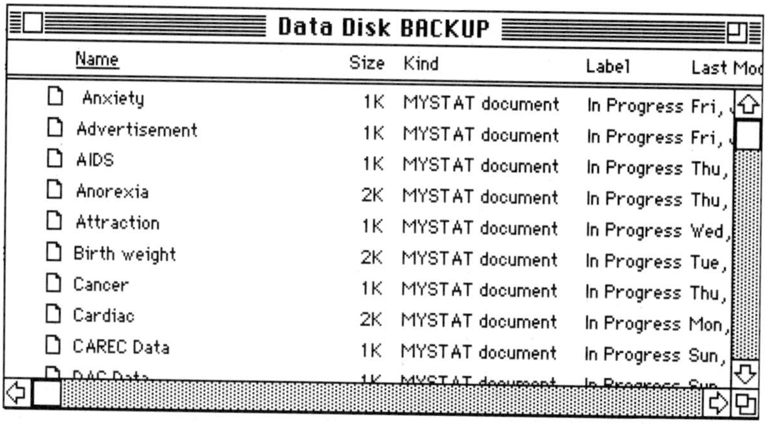

Figure 1.4
The contents of the Data Disk BACKUP

Name	Size	Kind	Label	Last Mod
Anxiety	1K	MYSTAT document	In Progress	Fri,
Advertisement	1K	MYSTAT document	In Progress	Fri,
AIDS	1K	MYSTAT document	In Progress	Thu,
Anorexia	2K	MYSTAT document	In Progress	Thu,
Attraction	1K	MYSTAT document	In Progress	Wed,
Birth weight	2K	MYSTAT document	In Progress	Tue,
Cancer	1K	MYSTAT document	In Progress	Thu,
Cardiac	2K	MYSTAT document	In Progress	Mon,
CAREC Data	1K	MYSTAT document	In Progress	Sun,

12. After all the files have been copied, drag the Data Disk and the MYSTAT Program and Data disk icons onto the Trash icon. The Trash icon will darken and the disks will be ejected when you release the mouse button. Put the original MYSTAT Program and Data disk in a safe place.

You will be using MYSTAT on the hard disk and the Data Disk (which will be called simply the *data disk* from now on) in the floppy disk drive.
Skip to the section "Starting MYSTAT" on page 9.

Floppy Disk Installation

If you do not have a hard disk, you need two 800K floppy disk drives to use MYSTAT. First, you'll copy the MYSTAT program files to a floppy disk, then you'll create a data disk that can also start up your Macintosh.

To install MYSTAT on a floppy disk,

1. Start with the Macintosh turned off.
2. Insert the Systems Tools disk, which comes with the Macintosh, into one of the floppy drives.
3. Turn the computer on.
4. Once the system is running, get two unitialized floppy disks. Label one blank floppy *MYSTAT Program Disk*, and label the other one *Data Disk and Startup*.
5. Insert the MYSTAT Program Disk into the other floppy disk drive. A dialog box like the one shown in Figure 1.5 will appear.

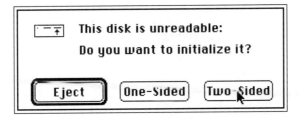

Figure 1.5
The disk initialization dialog box

6. Click **Two-Sided**. A message will appear warning you that this process will erase all information on the disk.
7. Click **Erase**.
8. The system now asks you to name this disk. Type **MYSTAT Program**, and click **OK**. When the initialization is complete, the icon for this disk will appear on the screen.
9. Eject the MYSTAT Program Disk by dragging the disk icon onto the Trash icon. The Trash icon will darken and the disk will be ejected when you release the mouse button.
10. Repeat steps 5–9 to initialize the Data Disk and Startup disk.

You are now ready to copy the MYSTAT program files to the MYSTAT Program Disk.

1. Eject the System Tools disk by dragging its icon to the trash. Its icon will remain on the screen.

2. Make sure the original MYSTAT Program and Data disk that comes with this book is locked then insert it into one drive. Insert your MYSTAT Program Disk into the other drive.
3. Double-click on the MYSTAT Program and Data disk icon. You will see a window like the one shown in Figure 1.6.

☞ If the Macintosh prompts you to switch disks during the copying process, follow the instructions on the screen.

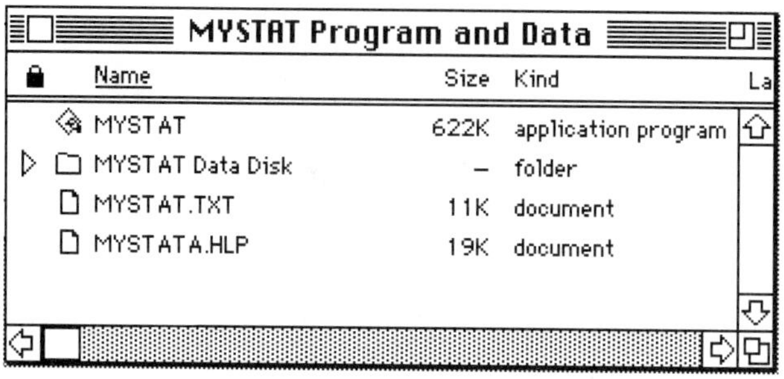

Figure 1.6
The contents of the MYSTAT Program and Data disk

	Name	Size	Kind
	MYSTAT	622K	application program
▷	MYSTAT Data Disk	—	folder
	MYSTAT.TXT	11K	document
	MYSTATA.HLP	19K	document

4. Press and hold down [**Shift**]. While holding [Shift] down, click on the files MYSTAT, MYSTATA.HLP, and MYSTAT.TXT. Let go of [**Shift**]. The three files should be highlighted in the window.
5. Drag the three files onto the MYSTAT Program Disk icon. The files will be copied to the MYSTAT Program Disk.
6. After the three files have been copied, double-click on the MYSTAT Program Disk and make sure that all three files are in it. The MYSTAT Program Disk window should look similar to Figure 1.7. Your screen may look different if an option other than **by Name** is checked in the **View** menu.

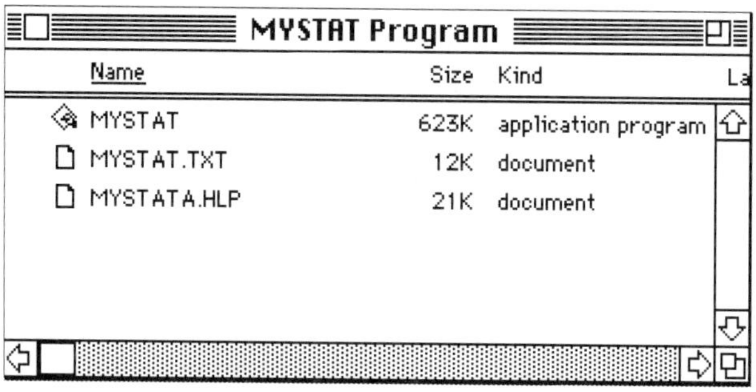

Figure 1.7
The contents of the MYSTAT Program Disk

Name	Size	Kind
MYSTAT	623K	application program
MYSTAT.TXT	12K	document
MYSTATA.HLP	21K	document

7. Drag the MYSTAT Program Disk icon to the Trash to eject it.

Now you need to copy the data files to the Data Disk and Startup disk.

1. Insert the Data Disk and Startup disk into the empty floppy disk drive.
2. Double-click on the MYSTAT Data Disk folder icon in the MYSTAT Program and Data disk window.
3. Choose **Select All** from the **Edit** menu. All of the files in the MYSTAT Data folder will be highlighted.
4. Drag the files onto the Data Disk and Startup icon to copy them to the Data Disk and Startup disk.

    You may be prompted to switch disks while the files are being copied. Follow the instructions on the screen.

5. Double-click on the Data Disk and Startup icon to make sure that the data files were copied. Your screen should look similar to Figure 1.8. Your screen may look different if an option other then **by Name** is checked in the **View** menu.

Figure 1.8
The contents of the Data Disk and Startup disk

Name	Size	Kind	Label	Last Mod
Anxiety	1K	MYSTAT document	In Progress Fri,	
Advertisement	1K	MYSTAT document	In Progress Fri,	
AIDS	1K	MYSTAT document	In Progress Thu,	
Anorexia	2K	MYSTAT document	In Progress Thu,	
Attraction	1K	MYSTAT document	In Progress Wed,	
Birth weight	2K	MYSTAT document	In Progress Tue,	
Cancer	1K	MYSTAT document	In Progress Thu,	
Cardiac	2K	MYSTAT document	In Progress Mon,	
CAREC Data	1K	MYSTAT document	In Progress Sun,	
DAC Data	1K	MYSTAT document	In Progress Sun,	

6. After all the files have been copied, drag the Data Disk and Startup and the MYSTAT Program and Data disk icons to the Trash. Put the original MYSTAT Program and Data disk in a safe place.

The Data Disk and Startup disk now contains the data files that you will need for the rest of this book. Next, you will copy some files from your System Tools disk to this disk.

☞ To complete the following steps you will need the System Tools disk, Utilities Disk 1, Utilities Disk 2, and the Printing Tools disk that come with the Macintosh. Make sure that all of these disks are locked.

8 Chapter 1 MYSTAT Overview

1. Insert the System Tools disk in one drive and the Data Disk and Startup disk into the other drive.
2. Double-click on the System Tools disk icon.
3. Double-click on the Installer icon. A dialog box saying "Welcome to the Apple Installer" appears.
4. Click **OK**. An Easy Install dialog box appears.
5. Click the **Customize** button. Your screen should look similar to the one in Figure 1.9.

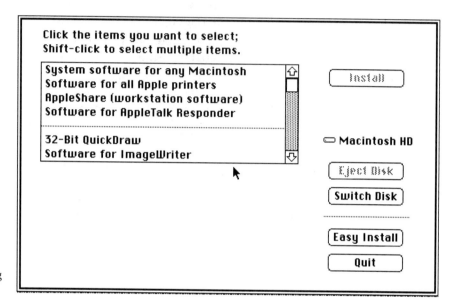

Figure 1.9
The Customize dialog box

6. Choose the name of your printing software by clicking on its name on the scrollable list shown in Figure 1.9.
7. Scroll down the list to find the *minimal* software for the Macintosh you are using. For example, if you are working on a Macintosh Plus, find "Minimal Software for Macintosh Plus." Press and hold [**Shift**] down, then click on the software name while you are holding down [Shift]. Let go of [**Shift**].

   You should see a list of your selections in the lower-left corner of the screen. Make sure it indicates that you have selected a printer and a minimal software configuration for your Macintosh.
8. Click **Install** and the system will install startup system files onto the Data Disk and Startup disk.
9. Follow the instructions on your screen. After the installation is complete, you will see a message saying that the installation was successful. Click **Quit**. (If you don't get this message,

you may need to choose different options under the Customize feature. See your instructor for help.)

10. Eject the disks by dragging their icons to the Trash icon. Put the System Tools disks away.
11. Select **Restart** from the **Special** menu.
12. Insert the Data Disk and Startup disk into the first drive.
13. After the computer has restarted, insert the MYSTAT Program Disk disk into the second drive.

    ☞ From now on, repeat step 12 before you turn on your Macintosh, then repeat step 13 after the system has started.

14. Select Chooser from the menu. You should see the name of the printer that you chose during the customized installation in the window in the upper-left corner.
15. Click once on the printer icon to select it, then click the close box in the upper-left corner of the title bar to close the Chooser window.

You will be using the MYSTAT Program Disk, which will be called MYSTAT from now on, in one floppy drive, and the Data Disk and Startup disk, which will be called simply the *data disk* from now on, in the other floppy drive.

■ Starting MYSTAT

Do the following steps to start MYSTAT.

1. Make sure that the data disk is not locked and is in a floppy disk drive. If you do not have a hard disk, make sure that the MYSTAT Program Disk is in the other floppy drive.

   WARNING: *To run MYSTAT on a system without a hard disk, both the MYSTAT Program Disk and Data Disk and Startup disk may not be locked.*

2. If you have a hard disk, double-click on the MYSTAT Program folder. If you do not have a hard disk, double-click on on the MYSTAT Program Disk.
3. Double-click on the MYSTAT program icon (it's labeled MYSTAT). The copyright screen shown in Figure 1.10 will appear.
4. Click once in this copyright box.

Figure 1.10
MYSTAT copyright box

MYSTAT Menu Bar

After starting MYSTAT and clicking in the copyright screen, you will see a screen with the menu shown in Figure 1.11.

Figure 1.11
MYSTAT's seven menus

This menu bar illustrates MYSTAT's seven menus. While their use will be detailed throughout this book, a brief description of each follows.

File Menu

You open, close, and save data files with the **File** menu. You can print and save selected text and graphs, submit commands from a file or the Clipboard, and quit MYSTAT.

Edit Menu

The **Edit** menu contains commands for copying, cutting, and pasting information. It is also used for displaying the Clipboard contents.

Data Menu

The **Data** menu allows you to sort, rank, and standardize variables; redirect analysis output to the printer or a file; and control the format settings of the Analysis window.

Graph Menu

The **Graph** menu allows you to construct various scatterplots, histograms, box plots, series plots, and stem-and-leaf diagrams.

Analyze Menu

You will use the **Analyze** menu to compute all of the statistics discussed in this book. For each choice, MYSTAT presents a dialog box in which you select both the variables and the options that will be used in the analysis.

Goodies Menu

The **Goodies** menu provides an introduction to MYSTAT and information about SYSTAT. Other choices let you open the view and command windows and transfer to another application.

Editor Menu

The **Editor** menu offers items for working with the Data Editor for creating, changing, and deleting variables; finding cases; and generating random data.

■ MYSTAT Windows

MYSTAT uses four different windows: the Data Editor window, the View window, the Analysis (text-output window), and the Command window. All of the windows are resizable.

☞ The window you are working in is called the *active window*. You may switch between MYSTAT's windows any time by clicking in the window you want to make active.

Data Editor Window

You enter, create, display and edit data in the Data Editor window. Chapter 2 details these uses.

View Window

MYSTAT displays graphs in the View window. You can open and close this window with the **Show view window** and **Hide view window** commands from the **Goodies** menu.

Analysis Window

MYSTAT displays statistical output in the Analysis window. This window is titled "MYSTAT: A Personal version of SYSTAT." You may also add your own comments, cut and paste information, or reformat the results to write your own reports.

Commands Window

The optional Commands window is used with the Command Interface. Discussion of the Command Interface is beyond the scope of this book.

■ Obtaining Help

You can obtain on-screen help for MYSTAT in two ways.
1. Click the question mark **(?)** icon in the upper-left corner of any of MYSTAT's dialog boxes for help with that procedure.
2. Select **Help** from the **Editor** menu for help with the Data Editor.

■ Quitting MYSTAT

When you are finished working with MYSTAT, you should quit the program and shutdown the Macintosh.

WARNING: *Students in computer laboratories may be asked to leave the power on for the next student. Check with your lab instructor before continuing.*

1. Select **Quit** from the **File** menu.
2. Select **Shutdown** from the **Special** menu. The Macintosh will eject your disks. Take them with you when you leave.

2

Data Editor

Statisticians study data, collections of objects. Quantities that change and can be measured and studied in statistics are called variables. For example, the time spent by several individuals reading the first chapter in this tutorial is a variable. Variables may be *quantitative* (for example, age or weight) or *categorical* (for example, brands of cars or occupations). To conduct statistical calculations, variables need to be named so that their meaning and derivation can be easily remembered, and their values need to be recorded. Often to discover statistical patterns, new variables must be created mathematically or, more often, from other variables already collected. Finally, variables need to be saved to conduct future analyses. MYSTAT enables users to do all of this using the MYSTAT Data Editor window, the **Editor** menu, and the **Open**, **Save**, and **Save as...** commands.

Objectives

At the end of this tutorial you should be able to
- Recognize the MYSTAT Data Editor
- Enter data into MYSTAT from the keyboard
- Edit data
- Save data to a disk as either a MYSTAT file or a text file
- Create new variables with the **Math...**, **Recode...**, and **Find case...** commands
- Search for and find data values that meet specific conditions
- Read a text file
- Fill the Data Editor worksheet with a given number of null cases
- Know the functions of the **Sort...**, **Rank...**, and **Weight...** commands
- Know how to format data and analyses
- Know how to send output to the screen, the printer, or a disk file
- Use the Clipboard

■ The MYSTAT Data Editor

The Data Editor window is where data are entered into MYSTAT. Before beginning, make sure your printer is selected under the Chooser. For help selecting a printer refer to your Macintosh manuals or see your instructor.

1. Start MYSTAT by double-clicking on the MYSTAT icon.

WARNING: *If you do not have a print file installed in the System folder on the Startup disk, you will see the message shown in Figure 2.1. You must click on **OK** to continue. Without a print file installed in the System folder on the Startup disk, you will not be able to print. If you want to print, you will need to quit MYSTAT and install a print file. Refer to your Macintosh manual or see your instructor.*

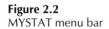

Figure 2.1
No print file dialog box

2. Click inside the window with the copyright notice.

The menu bar that now appears at the top of the computer screen (see Figure 2.2) lists all of the available menu choices.

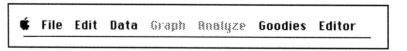

Figure 2.2
MYSTAT menu bar

Below the menu bar, you will see the MYSTAT Data Editor window. See Figure 2.3. Within this window, which looks very much like a spreadsheet, you will store both variable names and variable values to make a data set.

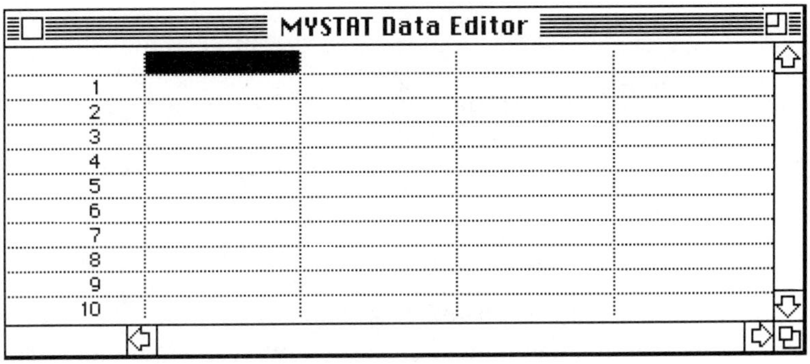

Figure 2.3
Empty Data Editor window

This is a typical Macintosh window and can be resized or moved. The rest of the Data Editor consists of rows of boxes called cells. MYSTAT requires you to name each variable in the first row before it lets you enter any values in a column. This first row, which we'll call the variable-naming row, is not numbered. Each subsequent row is numbered. These numbers tell how many cases or subjects are stored in the data set.

☞ The cell directly above the cell containing the number 1 is never used.

■ Keyboard Entry

The simplest method for entering data is from the keyboard. You will key in data that lists the 1985 populations (in thousands) and areas of the twenty largest cities in the world. You may be surprised to see how few U.S. cities are on the list. The data are listed in Table 2.1. Do not enter the data yet.

City	Population	Area
Tokyo	25434	1089
Mexico City	16901	522
Sao Paolo	14911	451
New York	14598	1274
Seoul	13665	342
Osaka	13562	495
Buenos Aires	10750	535
Calcutta	10462	209
Bombay	10137	95
Rio	10116	260
Moscow	9873	379
Los Angeles	9638	1110
London	9442	874
Paris	8633	432
Cairo	8595	104
Manila	8485	188

Table 2.1 cont.

Table 2.1
Population and area of the 20 largest cities in the world

City	Population	Area
Jakarta	8122	76
Essen	7604	704
Teheran	7354	112
Delhi	6993	138

Naming Variables

There are three variables in this data set. The first is the name of the city. This type of variable is often called a *text*, *ASCII*, or *character* variable because the values are expressed with alphabetic characters. In MYSTAT variable names always begin with a letter and can be up to eight characters long. Names of text variables must end with a $, which does not count as one of the eight characters.

The second variable, the population in 1985, must also be meaningfully abbreviated using eight or fewer characters. Since population is a *numeric* variable (the values are numbers) no special ending is required for the variable name. The third variable, the area of each city, is also numeric.

To name the variables for the population data,

1. Type **CITY$** into the first column of the variable-naming row in the MYSTAT Data Editor window, and press [**Return**].
2. Type **POP** in the second column of the variable-naming row. Press [**Return**].
3. Name the third variable by typing **AREA** in the third column of the variable-naming row. Don't forget to press [**Return**].

Your Data Editor window should look like Figure 2.4.

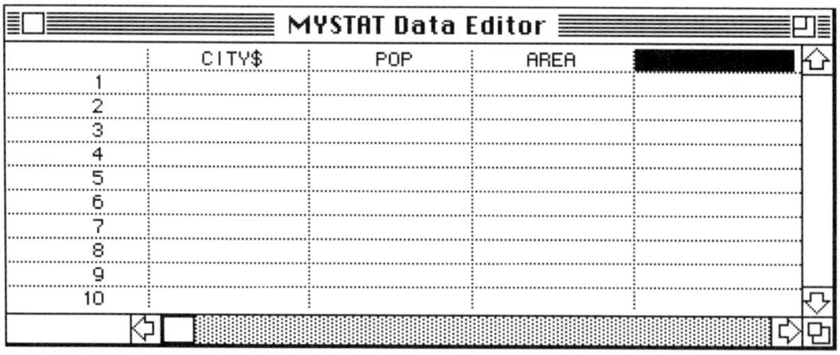

Figure 2.4
Data Editor window with three variables named

To enter values for the variables,

1. Use the mouse to place the cursor (the cursor will look like a cross) under CITY$ in the first numbered row and click once.

The cell in the first numbered row, first column will darken. You may now type in the character value of that variable.

Character values can be up to twelve letters long. MYSTAT differentiates between capital and lowercase letters, so *Tokyo* and *tokyo* would be two distinct entries.

> ☞ If you don't have a value for a text variable, you may type in a double or single quote followed by a blank space and then press [Return] to indicate the missing value. Another method for skipping over a cell is to use the mouse to highlight the next cell.

2. Type **Tokyo** and press [**Return**].

   MYSTAT enters this value and moves to and highlights the first cell under POP.

   WARNING: *If your MYSTAT disk is write protected (see chapter 1), you will get an error message. After pressing [Return], the program will stop. You must work with an unlocked disk.*

3. Type **25434** and press [**Return**].

   This value will be displayed as 25434.000. The Data Editor default display is three decimal places.

   Numeric variables may not have more than twelve digits before or after the decimal place and they may not have more than fifteen digits total. You must enter very large or small numbers using scientific notation. Variable values may not be larger than 10^{35}. If a numeric value is missing, you can type in a period (.) to indicate that it is missing.

   The first cell under AREA should now be active.

4. Type **1089** and press [**Return**].

   You automatically are moved to the next active cell in the second row under CITY$.

5. Fill in the rest of the variable values using the values given in Table 2.1.

   When you enter the four numbers in the tenth row, your Data Editor window will scroll so that you can enter the eleventh case. You can move back to the top by using the scroll bar on the right side of the window. You can move right or left in the Data Editor window by using the scroll bar on the bottom of the window.

   After scrolling back to the top of the screen, your completed data set should look like Figure 2.5.

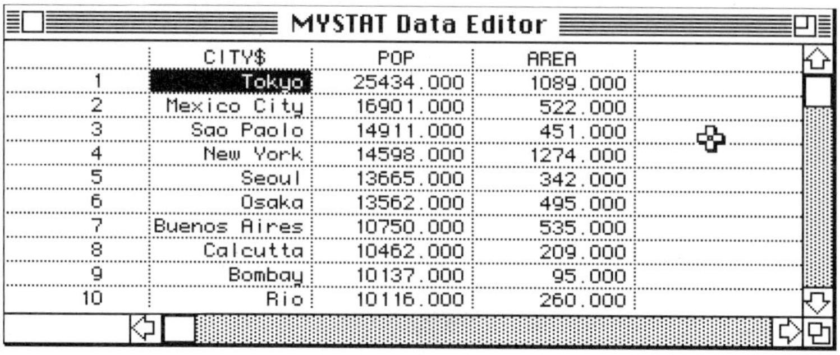

MYSTAT Data Editor

	CITY$	POP	AREA
1	Tokyo	25434.000	1089.000
2	Mexico City	16901.000	522.000
3	Sao Paolo	14911.000	451.000
4	New York	14598.000	1274.000
5	Seoul	13665.000	342.000
6	Osaka	13562.000	495.000
7	Buenos Aires	10750.000	535.000
8	Calcutta	10462.000	209.000
9	Bombay	10137.000	95.000
10	Rio	10116.000	260.000

Figure 2.5
Completed Data Editor window

■ Editing Data

If you notice an error in the data, you may place the cursor in the cell with the error and click once. Then type the correct value and press either [Return], [Enter], or an arrow key. The new value will replace the old value. If you make an error before you complete an entry, back up by pressing the [Delete] key and reenter the correct value.

You can delete the data in a row or column by clicking on the row number to select a row or double-clicking on the variable name to select a column. Then press ⌘–X (hold down the ⌘ key and press X simultaneously). Be careful! Once the data are removed, they are gone forever.

To practice deleting a row, complete the following steps:

1. Click on the number **1** in the first row to select the values for Tokyo.

   The Data Editor should look like Figure 2.6.

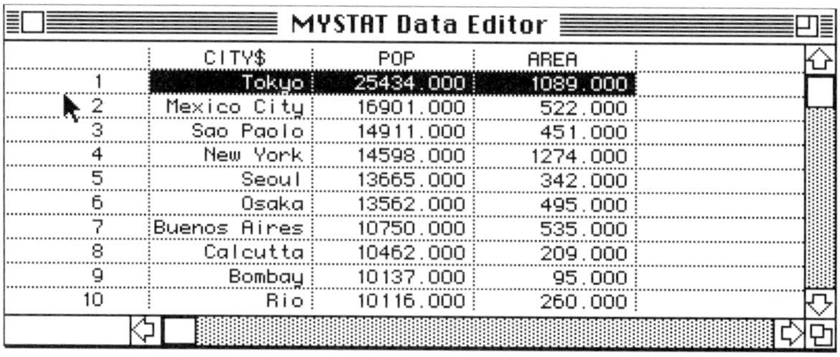

MYSTAT Data Editor

	CITY$	POP	AREA
1	Tokyo	25434.000	1089.000
2	Mexico City	16901.000	522.000
3	Sao Paolo	14911.000	451.000
4	New York	14598.000	1274.000
5	Seoul	13665.000	342.000
6	Osaka	13562.000	495.000
7	Buenos Aires	10750.000	535.000
8	Calcutta	10462.000	209.000
9	Bombay	10137.000	95.000
10	Rio	10116.000	260.000

Figure 2.6
Selecting an entire row

2. Press **⌘–X**.

   The data in the row will be deleted. The Data Editor now looks like Figure 2.7.

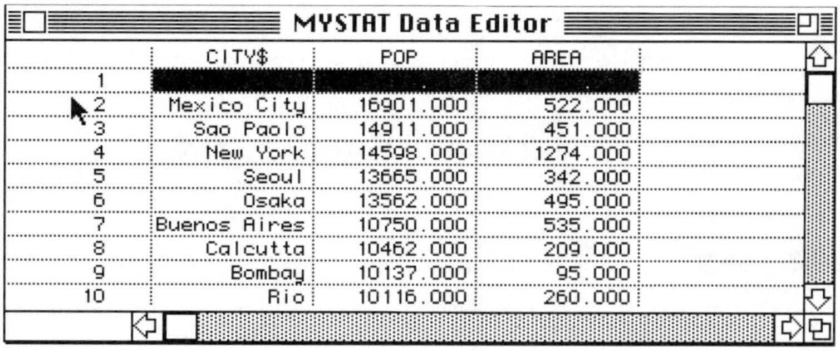

Figure 2.7
Data Editor after the first row of data has been deleted

	CITY$	POP	AREA
1			
2	Mexico City	16901.000	522.000
3	Sao Paolo	14911.000	451.000
4	New York	14598.000	1274.000
5	Seoul	13665.000	342.000
6	Osaka	13562.000	495.000
7	Buenos Aires	10750.000	535.000
8	Calcutta	10462.000	209.000
9	Bombay	10137.000	95.000
10	Rio	10116.000	260.000

3. Reenter the Tokyo data in the row.

You can also delete an entire row or column, not just the data. After selecting a row or column, use the Delete key instead of the ⌘–X key combination. If you delete a row, each row below the deleted row will move up one row. If you delete a column, each column to the right of the deleted column will move left one column. Because you cannot insert a row or column between existing rows or columns using MYSTAT, you would have to reenter the deleted data in the last row or column.

■ Saving Data

Always save your data after making changes. Under the **File** menu, there are two choices for saving data, **Save** and **Save as...**. If you choose the **Save** command the first time you save data, the data set automatically will be named *MYSTAT Data Editor*. The **Save as...** command allows you to save the data with a name you provide. After you have named a file once, any modifications to the file can be saved with the **Save** command and the name will stay the same.

If you try to save a new data set with the same name as a previous data set, you will be asked if the current data should replace the old data. If you click in the [Yes] box, the older file will be erased and the new one will replace it.

☞ If you make a mistake and choose the **Save** command the first time you save a file, you can rename it after you quit MYSTAT.

To save data for the first time, use the following steps:

1. Make sure the data disk is in the drive.

20 *Chapter 2   Data Editor*

2. Choose the **Save as...** command under the **File** menu.

WARNING: *Do not select **Save selected text as...** command.*

3. Click once in the **Drive** button.

   The drive button toggles back and forth between your computer's disk drives. (The figures in this book show a Macintosh with a hard drive called HD1 and the Data Disk BACKUP disk in the floppy drive.) You will save all your data files to your data disk. If your window does not indicate that you are saving the file to your data disk, then click in the **Drive** button until Data Disk is selected.

   The dialog box like the one shown in Figure 2.8 should be on your screen.

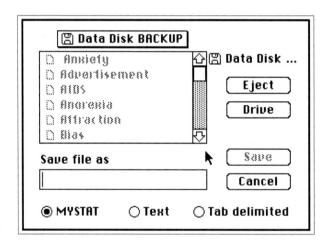

Figure 2.8
Save as... dialog box

4. Type **Cities** in the box headed by "Save file as."
5. Click once on the **Save** button. A window like that in Figure 2.9 appears.
6. Click once on **OK**.

   MYSTAT saves the twenty-five cases to your data disk.

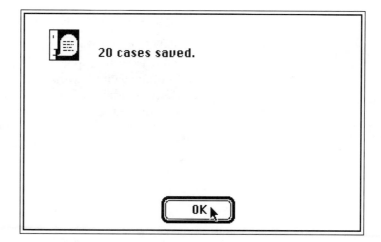

Figure 2.9
Save notification

☞ The three buttons at the bottom of the **Save as** dialog box (see Figure 2.8) allow you to save the data in MYSTAT format (the default), as Text (each entry is separated by a comma, and character values are surrounded by quotes), or as Tab delimited (the data set is saved as text but the entries are separated by tabs instead of commas). The Text option is useful if you want to import the data set into your word-processing program. The Tabs option is useful if you need to import the data set into a spreadsheet program. Usually, you will use the default option and save the data set in a MYSTAT format.

■ Transforming Data

It is often necessary to create new variables or transform (re-express) existing variables. Frequently a new variable must be generated from one or more previously stored variables. In this tutorial you will create two new variables by typing two new names in the variable-naming row. For the first new variable, you will use the **Math...** command under the **Editor** menu to calculate all of the first variable's values. The **Math** command allows you to re-express the value of a variable (for example, square root the values). For the second variable, you will use the **Recode...** command under the **Editor** menu to create the text values. The **Recode** command allows you to add conditions (*if... then*) when you re-express values.

Using the Math... Command

First, we'll calculate the number of people per square mile in each city. These values can be found by dividing the city's population (POP) by the city's area (AREA) and multiplying by 1,000.

To accomplish this, complete these steps:

1. Select the **Math...** command from the **Editor** menu.

   The dialog box in Figure 2.10 appears. Notice the box in the upper left where all the available variables appear, the box in the upper right where several math functions can be selected, (see the Odds and Ends section at the end of this chapter for a complete description of all the Functions), and an area in the lower portion of the window above the **OK**, **Cancel**, and **Clear** buttons where the mathematical equation is written. In the upper-left hand corner of the dialog box is an icon that identifies this as the **Math** dialog box. Below the **Math** icon is a question mark. Clicking once on the question mark will provide on-screen help about the **Math...** command.

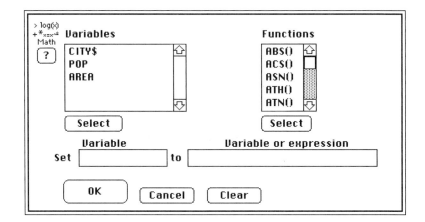

Figure 2.10
Math... dialog box window

To complete the dialog box, perform the following steps:

2. Type **DENSITY** in the "Set Variable" box.
3. Click in the "Variable or expression" box.
4. Double-click on **POP** in the "Variables" box.
5. Type the divide sign (/) in the " to Variable or expression" box.
6. Double-click on **AREA** in the "Variables" box.

   The completed dialog box looks like Figure 2.11.

7. Click **OK** to create the new variable values.

   Your new data set should look like Figure 2.12.

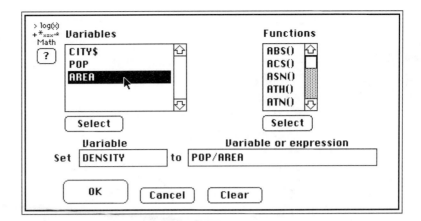

Figure 2.11
Completed **Math...**
dialog box

Figure 2.12
Completed Data
Editor window

Notice that Bombay is the densest city shown in the window. If you scroll down, you will see that Jakarta is even denser—almost ten times more people per square mile than New York!

Using the Recode... Command

Suppose you are trying to decide which cities are "huge" and which are simply "big." You could generate another set of variable values to indicate your decision. The **Recode** command under the **Editor** menu allows the use of "*If* condition *then* action" clauses.

You are going to create a new character variable. After you have set up a proper *If* condition *then* action equation, MYSTAT will input the value *Big* if the population is less than 10 million. After constructing a second equation, MYSTAT will input *Huge* for the variable value if the population is equal to or greater than 10 million.

Recode... works with both character and numeric variables. For small data sets it might be faster to type in the new variable values yourself. If you have a large data set, it is faster and more efficient to let MYSTAT do the work.

To create and code the new variable, use the scroll bar to locate the first empty column, and then complete the following steps:

1. Choose the **Recode** command from the **Editor** menu.

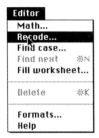

 After choosing the **Recode...** command, you will see a dialog box like Figure 2.13.

 We need to create an expression that says, "If POP is less than 10,000, then set SIZE$ equal to the word *Big*."

2. Double-click on the **POP** variable.

 This will place that name in the "If Test variable" box.

3. Select the less than button (**<**) by clicking on it once.

4. Click once in the top "Variable or expression" box and type the number **10000** (remember, these data are expressed in thousands).

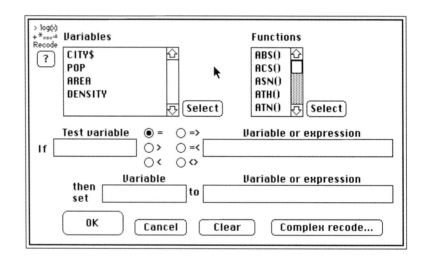

Figure 2.13
Recode... dialog box window

5. Click in the "then set Variable" box, and type **SIZE$**.

6. Click once in the "to Variable or expression" box and type in the value **"Big"**. Note that character values must have quotation marks around them.

 The completed dialog box window should look like Figure 2.14.

7. Click **OK**.

Transforming Data   25

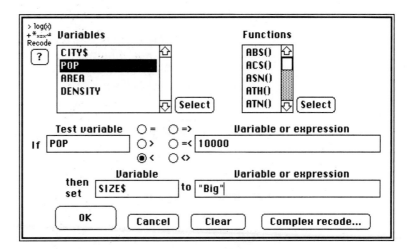

Figure 2.14
Completed **Recode...** dialog box for "Big"

You are now halfway through creating the values for the SIZE$ variable. Next you need to create the equation for the huge cities.

1. Choose **Recode...** again.
2. This time set the **Recode** function to say: If POP is equal to or greater than (=>) 10000, then set SIZE$ to the word *Huge*.

   Before clicking **OK**, your dialog box window should look like Figure 2.15.

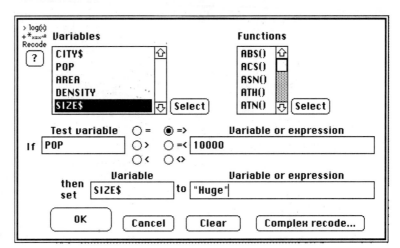

Figure 2.15
Completed **Recode...** dialog box for "Huge"

3. Click **OK**.

   Now you need to make the Editor window larger so that you can see all five columns.

4. Click on the resize button (two overlapping boxes in the lower-right corner of the Editor window) and drag it to the right until the five columns containing data show in the window. You may need to scroll the window to the left first to make sure the first column is showing.

☞ If you have a larger screen, you can also drag the resize button down to see all the cases.

Your data will look like Figure 2.16.

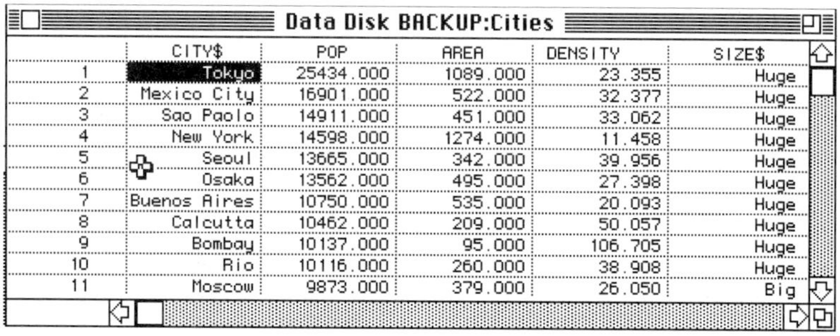

Figure 2.16
Completed **Recode...** command in the Data Editor window

	CITY$	POP	AREA	DENSITY	SIZE$
1	Tokyo	25434.000	1089.000	23.355	Huge
2	Mexico City	16901.000	522.000	32.377	Huge
3	Sao Paolo	14911.000	451.000	33.062	Huge
4	New York	14598.000	1274.000	11.458	Huge
5	Seoul	13665.000	342.000	39.956	Huge
6	Osaka	13562.000	495.000	27.398	Huge
7	Buenos Aires	10750.000	535.000	20.093	Huge
8	Calcutta	10462.000	209.000	50.057	Huge
9	Bombay	10137.000	95.000	106.705	Huge
10	Rio	10116.000	260.000	38.908	Huge
11	Moscow	9873.000	379.000	26.050	Big

Using the **Complex recode** button in the dialog box (shown in Figure 2.15), you can combine several recode commands. While this tutorial does not cover complex recodes until later, the interested student is encouraged to experiment.

5. Select **Save** under the **File** menu. You will be using this file later.

■ Finding Specific Cases

Often in statistical research, cases with specific values for variables need to be found. Obviously, in a small data set like the one we just created, it is quite easy to look at the values to see if a particular value for a variable exists. However, for larger data sets, MYSTAT has a function that quickly finds values.

Suppose you wished to find all the cities with more than 100,000 people per square mile. Do the following:

1. Scroll all the way to the top left in the Data Editor window, and click on **Tokyo**.

   This makes sure you start at the top of the data and will find all the cases.

Finding Specific Cases **27**

2. Choose the **Find case...** command under the **Editor** menu.

   You are presented with a dialog box like the one in Figure 2.17

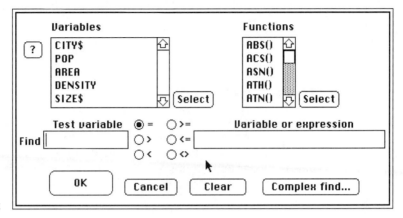

Figure 2.17
Find case... dialog box

To complete the dialog box, perform these steps:

3. Double-click on **DENSITY** in the "Variables" box. DENSITY appears in the "Find Test variable" box.
4. Click once on the greater than (**>**) button.
5. Click once in the "Variable or expression" box and type **100**.

   The completed dialog box should look like Figure 2.18.
6. Click **OK**.

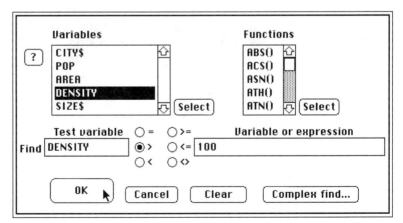

Figure 2.18
Dialog box for the
Find case... command

You are asking MYSTAT to find the next case in which DENSITY is greater than 100 (that is, 100,000 people per square mile). When you click **OK**, the first cell that meets this condition is highlighted. This city is Bombay. To find the next case, repeat the procedure or simply choose the **Find Next** command under the **Editor** menu.

28 Chapter 2 Data Editor

☞ The **Find Next** selection can be made with the menu and the mouse or by holding down the command key (⌘) and the N keys at the same time (⌘–N). It is easy to step through the data set by repeatedly pressing the ⌘–N key combination.

If you have a Macintosh with a large screen, resize the window so that you don't have to scroll left after each **Find Next** command.

■ Reading Text Files

Instead of typing data by hand, statisticians often read in data that have been saved by other researchers for other computer programs (often on other computer systems) in a text format. Text format is frequently used to transfer data from one computer system to another. On the data disk, there is a relatively large data set saved in a text format. It is titled "IQ Data in Text Format."

Try reading a file saved in that format now.

1. Choose the **Open** command under the **File** menu.
2. Make sure the data disk is selected. You may need to click in the **Drive** button.
3. Click in the **Text** button in the lower-right corner of the dialog box. You now should see the dialog box similar to the one in Figure 2.19.

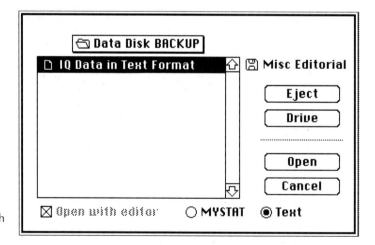

Figure 2.19
Open dialog box with **Text** format chosen

☞ The name of the data set only becomes visible when you click the **Text** button. When the **MYSTAT** button is selected only MYSTAT files are shown.

4. Double-click on the data set's name, or click once on the **Open** button.

A box appears that says, "Reading line..." and gives the line number currently being read. There are 200 lines to be read. The screen shown in Figure 2.20 appears after a short wait.

	COL01	COL02	COL03	COL04
1	3.000	1.000	1.000	85.000
2	2.000	2.000	2.000	98.000
3	3.000	3.000	3.000	84.000
4	1.000	4.000	4.000	65.000
5	1.000	5.000	4.000	45.000
6	3.000	6.000	1.000	92.000
7	3.000	7.000	1.000	80.000
8	3.000	8.000	4.000	64.000
9	3.000	9.000	5.000	103.000
10	3.000	10.000	5.000	92.000

Figure 2.20
Text file read into the Data Editor window

You have just read in a data set containing psychological test information on 200 children referred for a psychological evaluation. By scrolling through this data set, you will discover that it has thirteen variables and 200 cases. Since the names of the variables were unknown, MYSTAT simply named them COL01, COL02, COL03, and so on. In this data set all the variables are numeric.

When school children are referred for a psychological examination, they are given a battery of tests, including intelligence tests and achievement tests. Often behavior is also measured. Then the regular education teacher, special education teacher, parents, school administrator, and psychologist meet as a multidisciplinary team (MDT) to discuss the child. If the child needs special education, it is decided in this meeting. This data set contains information concerning 200 children after the MDT meeting was held.

The names of the variables are not very descriptive, so you should give them meaningful names. The first variable is the group assignment the multidisciplinary team gave the child. Only numbers were recorded. Children assigned to group 1 were assessed as trainable mentally retarded. Group 2 children were reported as emotionally disturbed and withdrawn. Group 3 children are nonhandicapped. Group 4 children are learning disabled. Group 5 children are emotionally disturbed and aggressive. Group 6 children are bright average. There is only a single child in group 7. This child (case 182) is discussed later.

Call the first variable MDT.

1. Click in the **COL01** cell and type **MDT**; then press **[Return]** or the right arrow [→] key.

The second variable is the child's identification number. This variable is a number from 1 to 200.

2. The cell **COL02** should be highlighted. Type **ID** to name this variable, and press **[Return]**.

The third variable is the group assignment the school psychologist gave the child. The psychologist did not always agree with the MDT decision.

3. Type **PSYCH** in the cell **COL03**, then press **[Return]** to name this variable.

The fourth variable is the child's Verbal IQ. This variable measures how children respond to verbal questions.

4. In cell **COL04**, type **VIQ** to name this variable.
5. Finish typing in each of the variable names as given below.

The fifth variable is the child's Performance IQ (**PIQ**). Performance IQs measure how children perform on test questions that are more visual than verbal.

The sixth variable is the child's Full Scale IQ (**FSIQ**). The FSIQ is a combination of the child's VIQ and PIQ.

The next three variables are the child's reading, spelling, and arithmetic scores. You can abbreviate these variables **READ**, **SPELL**, and **ARITH**.

The tenth and eleventh variables are behavioral scores. The first variable indicates how many points the child received on an aggressiveness scale. Abbreviate this variable as **AGGRESS**. The second variable indicates how withdrawn the teacher perceives the child to be in the classroom. Abbreviate this variable as **WITHDRAW**.

The twelfth and thirteenth variables are the child's **AGE** (in months) and **GRADE** in school.

When you are finished editing this data set, use the scroll bars to return to the first column. Your file should look like Figure 2.21.

	MDT	ID	PSYCH	VIQ
1	3.000	1.000	1.000	85.000
2	2.000	2.000	2.000	98.000
3	3.000	3.000	3.000	84.000
4	1.000	4.000	4.000	65.000
5	1.000	5.000	4.000	45.000
6	3.000	6.000	1.000	92.000
7	3.000	7.000	1.000	80.000
8	3.000	8.000	4.000	64.000
9	3.000	9.000	5.000	103.000
10	3.000	10.000	5.000	92.000

Figure 2.21
Completed text file in the Data Editor window

6. Finally use the **Save...** command and save the data set to the data disk as **School Referrals**. (Save it in MYSTAT format.) See Figure 2.22. You will be using this data set in later chapters.

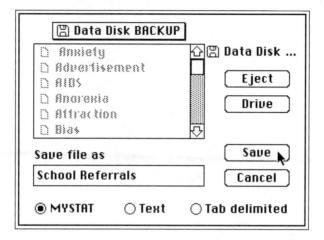

Figure 2.22
Saving the *School Referrals* file

■ A Special Note on Printing Data Sets

One feature not incorporated into MYSTAT is a direct command to print the data set. There is a procedure that will allow you to send the data set to the printer. We will be printing data sets in chapter 4, "Descriptive Statistics."

■ Odds and Ends

Functions, Relations, and Operators

Recall that in the **Math...**, **Recode...**, and **Find case...** dialog boxes, there are many mathematical functions, relations, and operators you can choose. We did not discuss them all, but you should know what they are. Below is a quick definition for each.

+	addition
−	subtraction
*	multiplication
/	division
^	exponentiation
>	greater than
<	less than
=	equal to
<>	not equal to
=>	equal to or greater than

32 *Chapter 2   Data Editor*

=<	equal to or less than
ABS	absolute value
ACS	arccosine
AND	logical and
ASN	arcsine
ATH	hyperbolic arctangent
ATN	arctangent
CASE	current case number
COS	cosine
EXP	exponential function
INT	integer truncation
LOG	natural logarithm (base e)
OR	logical or
SIN	sine (argument in radians)
SQR	square root
TAN	tangent
URN	uniform random number (0,1)
ZCF	standard normal cumulative density function
ZIF	inverse normal cumulative density function
ZRN	normal random number (0,1)

Filling the Worksheet

Sometimes you may need to calculate a statistic and you don't have a data set to enter into MYSTAT. The **Fill worksheet** command under the **Editor** menu allows users to fill a specified number of cases in a new worksheet with missing data values; later these missing values can be replaced with other values using the **Math** or **Recode** commands.

To do this,

1. Choose **New** from the **File** menu.

   The Data Editor will be cleared to produce a new file.

2. Type **SCORE** to name the first variable.

3. Choose **Fill Worksheet...** from the **Editor** menu.

   The dialog box shown in Figure 2.23 will appear.

4. Type 25, and click **OK**.

   The Data Editor will fill the SCORE variable with missing data (indicated by decimal points) for twenty five cases. You could now use the Math or Recode command to have these missing data values changed to numbers.

Odds and Ends   33

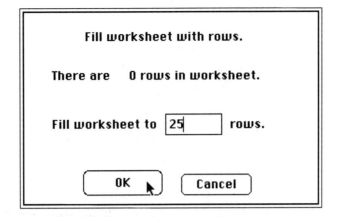

Figure 2.23
Fill Worksheet...
dialog box

The Sort, Rank, and Weight Commands

The **Data** menu has several commands that affect the Data Editor. The **Sort**, **Rank**, and **Weight** commands will be used later.

The **Sort** command sorts cases by one or more variables and creates a new sorted file. The cases are sorted in ascending order in the Data Editor (smallest numbers first). MYSTAT also allows for nested sorts. This means you can sort a list by one variable, then sub sort it by another, then by another, and so on. You may select up to ten numeric or text variables on which to do nested sorts. The sorted data are automatically saved in a new file on the disk. (To use this file, you will need to **Open** it with the MYSTAT program.)

Let's sort the *Cities* data to find the least and most densely populated cities.

To do this,

1. Select **Open** from the **File** menu.

    ☞ If you completed the last example, you may be asked if you want to "Save changes?" Click **No** to continue.

2. Click on the **Drive** button so that the contents of the data disk are listed.

3. Double-click on **Cities**. You may need to scroll down the list to see it.

4. Choose **Sort...** from the **Data** menu.

5. Double-click on **DENSITY** in the "Select sort variables" box.

    Your screen should look like Figure 2.24.

34 *Chapter 2   Data Editor*

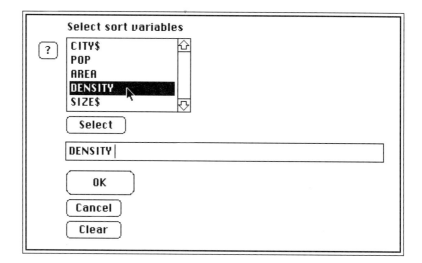

Figure 2.24
Sort... dialog box

6. Click **OK**.

   The dialog box shown in Figure 2.25 will appear.

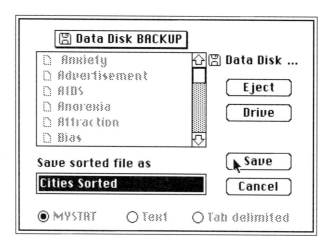

Figure 2.25
Sorted file dialog box

7. Click **OK** to save the sorted data in a file called *Cities Sorted*.
8. Open the file *Cities Sorted*.

   Your screen should look like Figure 2.26.

You can see that Los Angeles is the least densely populated city and Jakarta is the most densely populated.

Figure 2.26
Cities sorted by DENSITY

	CITY$	POP	AREA	DENSITY	SIZE$
1	Los Angeles	9638.000	1110.000	8.683	Big
2	Essen	7604.000	704.000	10.801	Big
3	London	9442.000	874.000	10.803	Big
4	New York	14598.000	1274.000	11.458	Huge
5	Paris	8633.000	432.000	19.984	Big
6	Buenos Aires	10750.000	535.000	20.093	Huge
7	Tokyo	25434.000	1089.000	23.355	Huge
8	Moscow	9873.000	379.000	26.050	Big
9	Osaka	13562.000	495.000	27.398	Huge
10	Mexico City	16901.000	522.000	32.377	Huge
11	Sao Paolo	14911.000	451.000	33.062	Huge

The **Rank** command produces a new data file in which the values of the chosen variable are replaced by their rank order. Tied ranks for selected variables are averaged.

The **Weight** command replicates cases by using the integer portions of the values of a weighting variable you select. The weighted data are used until you select the [Weighting off] option in the Weight dialog box window. This command does not change the data file, but it does affect subsequent statistical analyses. For example, if you entered the data set in Table 2.2 and chose the variable NUMBER as the weighting variable, the SCORE of 1 would be replicated nine times and the SCORE of 2 would be replicated eight times in any analysis.

Table 2.2
Sample data

SCORE	NUMBER
1	9
2	8
3	7
4	6

Formatting Input

MYSTAT lets you change the number of decimal places displayed in the Data Editor window.

1. Choose **Formats...** under the **Editor** menu.

   The dialog box shown in Figure 2.27 appears.

2. Click in the appropriate button for the number of decimal places you want displayed in the Data Editor window.

   This setting affects only what you see on the screen, not the precision of the data stored in the computer. MYSTAT stores at least fifteen digits for each number. Note that you may also select whether the cursor proceeds from left to right or from top to bottom when you press **[Return]**.

Figure 2.27
Changing the number of decimal places in the Data Editor

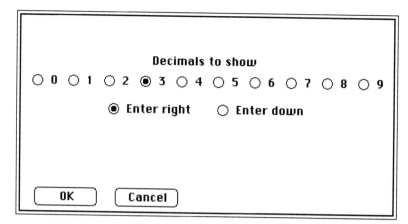

Formatting Output

MYSTAT allows you to format your output. If you select the **Formats...** command under the **Data** menu, you see the dialog box in Figure 2.28.

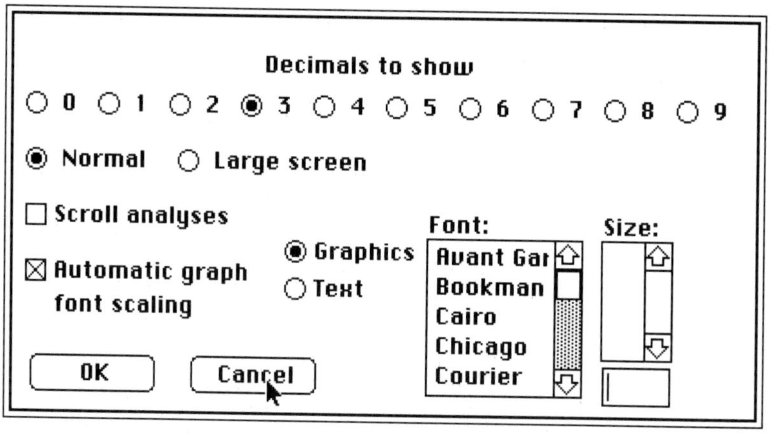

Figure 2.28
Formats... dialog box

With this dialog box, you control the number of decimals reported when statistical analysis results are presented in the Analysis window. In addition, you can elect to have the results of your analyses accumulated and scrolled in the Analysis window instead of having this window cleared after each separate analysis by checking the **Scroll analyses** box. Finally this command also allows you to select specific fonts for text and graphic output. Note, however, that you cannot change both text and graphics fonts at the same time. To change both, first change one, click **OK**, and then select **Format** again to change the other.

☞ The default choices here are typically best. For text output you should always choose nonproportional fonts, such as Monaco or Courier. Other fonts will ruin the orderly columns of output.

Directing Your Results

The last command under the **Data** menu is **Results to....** This command allows you to send statistical output to the screen, to the printer, or to a file on disk.

The default option is to send all output to your computer's screen (**Results to window**). If you want to print your graphs and statistical output, **Results to printer** must be chosen before analyses and graphs are done. If you do an analysis first and then choose **Results to printer**, nothing will happen. You must first choose **Results to printer** and subsequently do the analysis or graph.

Choosing **Results to file as** sends all subsequent statistical analyses to a text file. This is important if you are working with a word processor. Since all word processors can read text files, it will be quite easy to read this file and copy and paste it into the results section of your working paper.

☞ You cannot send graphs to a file as text. Graphs can be saved in a special format on a disk. This is discussed in the next chapter.

Using the Clipboard

You can also enter data into the Data Editor using the Clipboard **Paste** command. The data must be in the correct row and column format and all variable values must be separated by either commas, tabs, or spaces. Any text values that contain a space within them must be surrounded by a double or single quote.

WARNING: *You cannot do these steps now since the Clipboard is empty. This is not part of the tutorial but is presented here for advanced Macintosh users.*

To paste data from the Clipboard into the worksheet,

1. Place the cursor into the upper-left corner of the area you wish to fill. Click once to activate that cell.
2. Select the **Paste** command from the **Edit** menu.

To **Cut** or **Copy** data from a MYSTAT worksheet to the Clipboard,

1. Select the range of data you are interested in by placing the cursor in one corner of the data set while holding down the mouse button.
2. Drag the cursor diagonally to the opposite corner of the data set.
3. Release the mouse button and choose **Cut** or **Copy** from the **Edit** menu.

   For large data sets, Shift-Clicking works (see the Macintosh manual for details). If you used **Cut**, the selected cells will be filled with missing values. If you wish to cut or copy the entire data set instead of selected portions, the **Select all** command from the **Edit** menu will select all the cells.

Exercises

1. Figure 2.29 is a small data set containing information about the planets.

Figure 2.29 Planet data

	NAME$	DISTANCE	REVOLVE	DIAMETER
1	Mercury	36.000	88.000	3100.000
2	Venus	67.200	224.700	7700.000
3	Earth	92.900	365.260	7926.000
4	Mars	141.500	687.000	4200.000
5	Jupiter	483.400	4331.980	88700.000
6	Saturn	886.000	10760.560	75100.000
7	Uranus	1782.000	30685.490	29200.000
8	Neptune	2792.000	60194.850	27700.000
9	Pluto	3664.000	90474.902	3500.000
10				

Enter this data by keying it in. The variables indicate the name of the planet, it's DISTANCE from the sun, how many days it takes the planet to REVOLVE around the sun, and the DIAMETER of the planet.

2. Create a new variable that measures the time it takes each planet to revolve around the sun divided by the distance each is away from the sun. Is this value a constant? Save this data set as *Planets*.

3. Rank order the *Planets* data using both DISTANCE and DIAMETER as ranking variables. Save the ranked file as *Planets Ranked*. Open the *Planets Ranked* file and describe how the **Rank...** command changed the data set.

4. Open the *Planets* file. Sort the data using NAME$ as the sorting variable. Save the file as *Planets Sorted*. Open the *Planets Sorted* file and describe how the **Sort...** command changed the data set.

5. Data tabulated by Richard Heede of the Rocky Mountain Institute and reported in the March/April 1991 issue of *Sierra* magazine concerning federal spending on energy has been saved on your Data disk in a file titled *Taxpayers' Energy*. This data set lists energy in the United States from various sources and the money the federal government subsidized each source.

The variables are defined as follows: SOURCE$ is the energy source. BTU is the number of quadrillion British Thermal Units (a unit of heat) produced or saved by each source. SUBSIDY is the dollars in billions the federal government subsidizes each source. Finally, BTU_DOL is the number of BTUs each source provides per million dollars of expenditure by the government. Type in a new variable called DECISIN$ and use the following two statements to code the variable:

If BTU_DOL is less than 1.0, then set DECISIN$ to the word *Cut*.

If BTU_DOL is greater than or equal to 1.0, then set DECISIN$ to the word *Keep*.

You have just made decisions concerning energy sources to keep or cut from the federal budget. Be sure to save these data.

3

Graphing Data (Single Variables)

If a picture is worth a thousand words, a graph may be worth a thousand calculations when trying to summarize a large data set. Often, the human eye can detect subtleties within a graph that no amount of statistical analysis can disclose. The challenge for the researcher is producing accurate pictorial representations of data. If done correctly, graphs summarize and greatly speed our understanding of data. If done incorrectly, graphs can tell quite fanciful tales. MYSTAT provides several types of graphs that are helpful for visually representing single variables.

Objectives

At the end of this tutorial you should be able to
- Produce and print histograms, stem-and-leaf diagrams, and box plots
- Interpret typical scores (modality) and general shapes (skewness) of graphs
- Produce and print series graphs
- Change the size of a graph
- Move graphs in the View window
- Understand the basics of good graphic design

■ What Are Graphs?

A graph is a pictorial representation of one or more variables. Graphs are used to view and understand the shape of the *distribution* (frequency of all the values) of a variable. They also are used to visualize the relationship between two or more variables. This chapter will focus on one-variable graphs. Chapter 8 will discuss two variable graphs.

■ Histograms

A *histogram* is a graphical representation of the *density* or frequency of a single quantitative variable. It displays along the *x*-axis either single values or groups of values (*class intervals*). The height of each section of the histogram represents the frequency with which that value or class interval occurs. Unlike *bar charts*, in which the *x*-axis displays categories, the horizontal *x*-axis of a histogram shows a numeric scale.

A histogram is typically used to display the shape of a variable. However, a histogram's appearance can change depending upon the number of bars used. MYSTAT automatically chooses the best number of bars for revealing a variable's distribution. You may change this number if you wish.

Producing and Printing Histograms

Although a printout is often important, many reams of paper are wasted by indiscriminate printing. Wholesale printing is not necessarily helpful to understanding the data analysis, may be counterproductive (it takes time to print), and is objectionable on ecological grounds. Print only what you are assigned and only when necessary. Turn the print command off as soon as possible.

Let's produce and print the distribution of the population and density variables in the *Cities* data.

1. With MYSTAT running and the data disk in the floppy drive, select **Open** from the **File** menu.
2. Click on the **Drive** button so that the content of the data disk is listed.
3. Double-click on **Cities**.
4. Select **Results to printer** from the **Data** menu.

This will send the histograms you are about to produce to a printer attached to your computer.

WARNING: *If you do not want to print, omit step 1. If you inadvertently select* **Results to printer** *and do not want to print, you can select* **Results to window** *under the* **Data** *menu to turn the printing off.*

5. Select **Hist** from the **Graph** menu.

   You will see the dialog box in Figure 3.1, which offers additional options. For this histogram no options will be chosen, although we will discuss them.

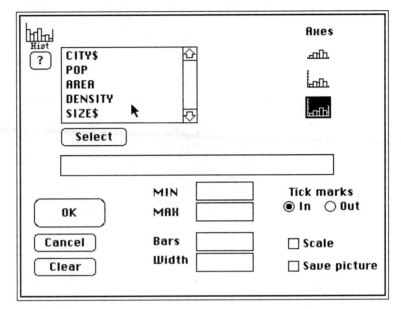

Figure 3.1
Histogram dialog box

In the box to the right of the question mark is a list of the variables in the data set; if more variables are available than can be shown in this area, the scroll bars on the right side will appear dark, indicating that you can scroll through for other variables. Clicking on a single variable in the variable box and then clicking on the **Select** button below chooses a variable for which a histogram will be constructed. You can also double-click on the variable you want to select. Selected variables are shown in the long rectangle below the **Select** button. If no variables are selected, MYSTAT will construct a histogram for every numeric variable in the data set.

In the upper right-hand corner are axes options. The horizontal x-axis displays the variable values. Vertical y-axes display frequencies in different scales. You can elect to have either a single x-axis plotted, an x- and y-axis, or an x- and two different y-axes (the default). For now, leave the default in effect.

The **MIN** and **MAX** options allow you to set the minimum and maximum values along the x-axis. You do not need to do this. MYSTAT selects these automatically for you. The **Bars** option lets you set the number of bars in the histogram. The **Width** option allows you to form intervals for continuous data. The number of bars chosen by MYSTAT is exemplary and users are unlikely to do better. The **Scale** option sets the *x*-axis to the minimum and maximum values found in the data, and the **Tick marks** buttons allow you to place the axes tick marks either just above the axes or below. Clicking the **Clear** button will clear all the selected options and allow you to start over. Clicking **Cancel** will stop the graphics procedure. Clicking **OK** will start the graphing.

6. Double-click on **POP** and **DENSITY** in the variables scroll list.
7. Click **OK**.

Whether you chose to send your results to the printer or to the window, the first histogram is drawn on your screen. If you chose **Results to printer**, you will then get a dialog box similar to the one shown in Figure 3.2.

Figure 3.2
The ImageWriter dialog box

In most cases you will want to accept the defaults, so

8. Click **OK**.

☞ You can also choose **Print graph...** from the menu. **Print graph...** prints the graph currently in the view window.

After the first histogram is drawn, you will see the alert shown in Figure 3.3.

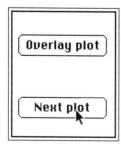

Figure 3.3
Overlay alert

If you choose **Overlay plot**, the next histogram will be drawn over the last one on the screen. If you choose **Next plot**, the old histogram is erased and the next one is drawn in a clean window. In most cases you will want to choose **Next plot**.

WARNING: *If you do not send the histograms to the printer or save them as PICT files (see the section on saving graphs later in this chapter), you cannot look at a previous graph once you have clicked **Next plot**.*

To draw the remaining histograms,

9. Click in the **Next plot** button.

Your histograms should look like those shown in Figure 3.4.

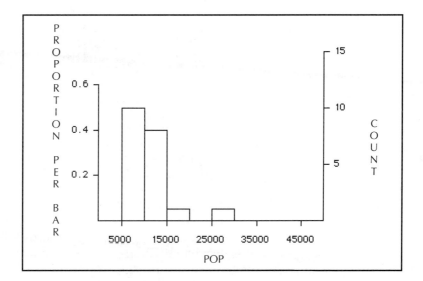

Figure 3.4a
Histogram of POP

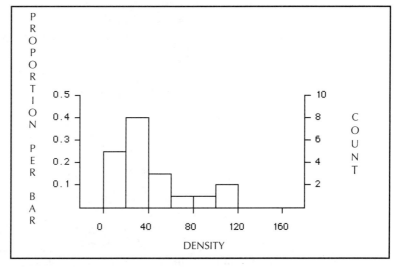

Figure 3.4b
Histogram of DENSITY

Among other things, histograms show the *skew* of a distribution, which is a measure of its symmetry. If a distribution is symmetric the left side of the distribution is a mirror image of the right side. If the values in a distribution bunch up at the smaller values, the distribution is positively skewed. If the distribution's values are predominately at the larger end of the scale, the distribution is negatively skewed. See Figure 3.5.

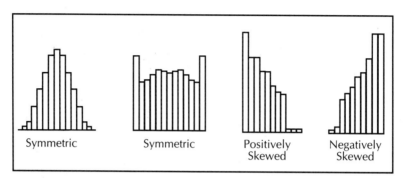

Figure 3.5
Skew of a distribution

In the histogram of populations (Figure 3.4a), the values of POP are scaled on the *x*-axis. MYSTAT groups the scores into equal-sized class intervals, and it labels selected intervals on the left side of the bar. The first class interval includes populations from 5 to 10 million. The second interval includes populations from 10 million to 15 million. The numbers on the left *y*-axis show the proportion of scores in each interval. The first interval (5,000,000 – 10,000,000) has a proportion of .5. Multiplying this proportion by 100 yields a percent. Thus, half of the cities have a population below 10 million. The *y*-axis on the right shows the number of cases per bar. The leftmost bar, cities below 10 million, contains 10 cities. Since there are 20 cities, this is half the sample. In the DENSITY histogram, the rightmost bar indicates cities with a density of 100,000 to 120,000 people per square mile. The right *y*-axis shows that only two cities fall into this category. Also note that both histograms are positively skewed.

■ Stem-and-Leaf Graphs

Stem-and-leaf displays are like histograms turned on their sides except that all or part of the values for each variable appear in the graph. To show how this is done, assume you have the following values for a variable:

[10, 11, 12, 13, 15, 17, 20, 22, 23, 25, 27, 30, 33, 33, 33, 34, 36, 38, 39]

These numbers can be broken into two parts called the *stem* and the *leaf*. For these values, the stem will be the first digit and the leaf the second digit. Thus, the score of 10 has a 1 as its stem and a 0 as its leaf. For the score 27, the 2 would be the stem and the 7 would be the leaf.

If you produced a histogram of the data it would look like Figure 3.6.

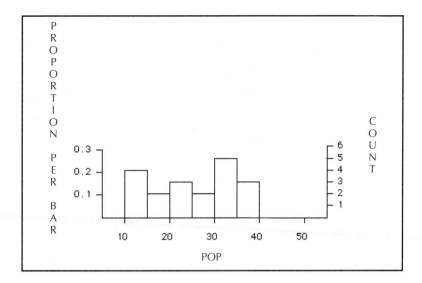

Figure 3.6
Histogram of variable SCORE

Note that the first class interval represented by the first bar in the histogram extends from 10 through 14, the second from 15 through 19, the third from 20 through 24, and so on. Each class interval is a bar in a histogram, and each of these bars becomes a row in a stem-and-leaf display. Each row in a stem-and-leaf display is headed by its stem and its length is determined by the number of leaves on the stem. For example, in creating the first row, we want to include all the numbers from 10 through 14 (10, 11, 12, 13). The stem for each of these numbers is 1 followed by the leaves 0123. The length of this row, which corresponds to the height of the bar in the histogram, is determined by the number of leaves following the stem. If the numbers from 15 through 19 are used for the second row, the stem will again be 1 and the leaves, 5 and 7. The only numbers within that class interval are 15 and 17. Note that each initial digit is used as a stem twice. Taking this to its conclusion, you get a stem-and-leaf display like that in Figure 3.7. Histogram bars have been superimposed over the leaves to show the similarity to a histogram. Note that if you rotate the stem-and-leaf diagram 90 degrees to the left, you see that the leaves look just like the histogram in Figure 3.6.

The advantage of the stem-and-leaf display over a histogram is that additional information (the actual variable values) is contained in the display. Additionally, MYSTAT will calculate the first, second, and third quartile scores, and mark the rows within which each occurs with a special symbol. The first and third quartile scores (the 25th and 75th percentile ranks) are also known as *hinges* and so an *H* is placed within the space between the stems and leaves to indicate the row in which these quartile scores fall. The second quartile is also known as the *median* (the score at the 50th percentile) and is marked with an *M*. If you enter the data above and produce the full stem-and-leaf output from MYSTAT, you would obtain the output shown in Figure 3.8.

Figure 3.7
Relationship between a stem-and-leaf display and a histogram

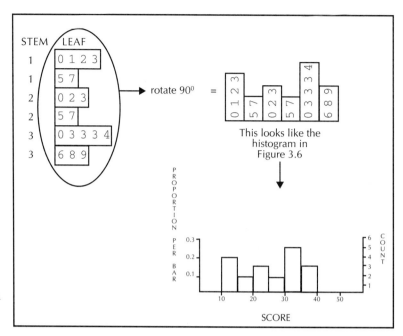

Figure 3.8
MYSTAT stem-and-leaf display

```
Stem and leaf plot of variable:   SCORE  ,  N = 19
Minimum is:              10.000
Lower hinge is:          16.000
Median is:               25.000
Upper hinge is:          33.000
Maximum is:              39.000

             1       0123
             1  H    57
             2       023
             2  M    57
             3  H    03334
             3       689
```

Using the *Cities* data set, stem-and-leaf plots can be produced for the population and density variable.

1. Load the *Cities* file from the data disk.
2. Select **Results to window** or **Results to printer** from the **Data** menu depending on where you want the output to appear.
3. Select **Stem** from the **Graph** menu.

The dialog box shown in Figure 3.9 will appear.

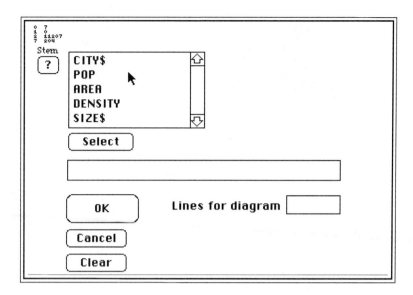

Figure 3.9
Dialog box for stem-and-leaf plots

The one new feature in this dialog box is the box labeled "Lines for diagram" in which you can indicate how many stems you want in the stem-and-leaf plot. Again, MYSTAT does a good job of making that decision, so this option is rarely used. If it is, however, simply type a number into the box.

4. Double-click on **POP** and **DENSITY**.
5. Click the **OK** button.

The two stem-and-leaf plots shown in Figure 3.10 will be generated.

Note that variables that are distant from the median are marked as outside values (see the stem-and-leaf displays). This is a useful measure for identifying values that stand apart from others. This frequently happens on one end when the distribution of a variable is seriously skewed. We will discuss how to determine when a data value is outside the expected values in the next section on box plots.

48 Chapter 3 Graphing Data

```
Stem and leaf plot of variable:    POP  ,  N =  20
Minimum is:         6993.000
Lower hinge is:        8540.000
Median is:          9994.500
Upper hinge is:       13613.500
Maximum is:        25434.000

             6    9
             7    36
             8 H  1456
             9 M  468
            10    1147
            11
            12
            13 H  56
            14    59
            15
            16    9
          ***Outside values***
            25    4
```

Figure 3.10a

```
Stem and leaf plot of variable:    DENSITY  ,  N =  20

Minimum is:          8.683
Lower hinge is:         20.039
Median is:           32.720
Upper hinge is:         50.366
Maximum is:         106.868


             0    8
             1    0019
             2 H  0367
             3 M  2389
             4    5
             5 H  00
             6    5
             7
             8    2
          ***Outside Values***
            10    66
```

Figure 3.10b

Box Plots

Box or box-and-whiskers plots display the distribution of a single variable. Figure 3.11 shows a typical box plot.

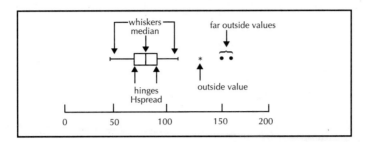

Figure 3.11
Typical box plot

In a box plot, the median of a variable is marked by a single vertical line. In this diagram, the median has a value of approximately eighty-three. The lower and upper hinges are the first and third quartiles (25th and 75th percentile ranks) respectively, and the distance between them is called the *Hspread*. The vertical lines that mark the hinges and the median are connected by horizontal lines to form a box The length of the box (the Hspread) is equivalent to the *interquartile range*, that is, fifty percent of the values fall within the box. The whiskers show how far the data spreads away from the hinges to a maximum distance of 1.5 Hspreads. If data values do not spread all the way to ±1.5 Hspreads from the hinges, the whiskers do not extend that far. Whiskers represent actual data points. Data values outside of the whiskers but less than three Hspreads from the hinges are marked with an asterisk. Data values more than three Hspreads from the hinges are marked by circles.

Let's examine the dialog box that appears when you select **Box** from the **Graph** menu with the *Cities* data file open in the Data Editor window.

To produce box plots for your four variables, follow these steps:

1. With the *Cities* filed loaded, choose **Box** from the **Graph** menu.

    You will see the dialog box shown in Figure 3.12. The "Grouping variable" box is new. You could select a variable in this box if that variable reflected subgroups of the full data; for example, if your data had scores for both males and females and a SEX variable coded these groups, you could produce separate box plots for males and females by selecting sex in the "Grouping variable" box. The axes selections determine the number of *x*- and *y*-axes drawn around the box plot. If you are creating box plots without a grouping variable only the default single *x*-axis option is allowed. If you are creating box plots with a grouping variable, the grouping variable is plotted on the *x*-axis while the values of the variable used to form the box plot are plotted on the *y*-axis.

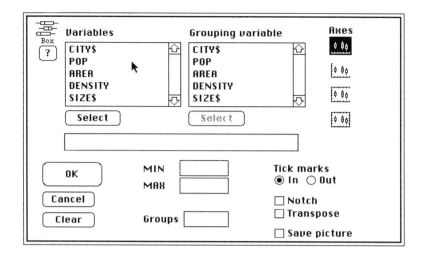

Figure 3.12
Box plot dialog box

Exercise 2 at the end of this chapter asks you to make grouped box plots. The "Notch" box produces notched box plots, which are discussed in chapter 11. For now leave this unchecked. The "Transpose" box rotates the direction of the box plot by 90 degrees. If the MIN and MAX values are set in this dialog box, it would be easy to directly compare the box plots that are generated.

2. Double-click on **POP**, then double-click on **DENSITY** in the "Variable" box.
3. Click **OK**.

The two box plots shown in Figure 3.13 are produced.

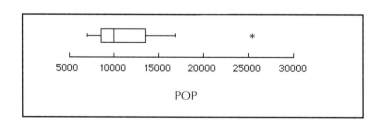

Figure 3.13a
Box plot of POP

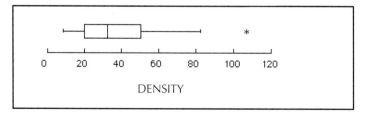

Figure 3.13b
Box plot of DENSITY

Again note that both variables are positively skewed.

☞ When using box plots, both skew and the outside values can be determined, but information may be lost concerning modality. However, bimodal distributions often produce large boxes with small whiskers.

■ Series Graphs

Occasionally you won't have a data set containing values from different people. You may have one that consists of a single subject who has been measured repeatedly. In such a situation, the case number does not constitute a different subject, but a time (a day, a week, or a month). The **Series** command under the **Graph** menu produces plots of a variable against time. It is especially useful for plotting single subjects. You can choose the **Standardize** option to change the variable's raw score values to z scores. A z score is a value which has the variable's mean subtracted from it. That result is divided by the standard deviation of the variable. Using z scores makes comparisons among the values easy. MYSTAT only plots the first fifteen cases unless you direct otherwise.

For example, if you were conducting a behavior modification experiment in which you were attempting to decrease a child's hitting behavior, the five-week baseline data (observations in which no intervention occurred) might be in rows 1–5 and the next ten cases might contain weekly observational data after the intervention program was introduced. A typical series graph produced by MYSTAT might look like Figure 3.14.

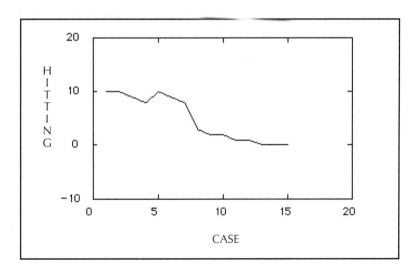

Figure 3.14
Series graph output

52 Chapter 3 Graphing Data

The following information would be displayed in the Analysis window. The Analysis window should be partly visible behind the graph. Click on it to see it fully.

Plot of HITTING

Number of cases =   15

Mean of series =   4.867

Standard deviation of series =   4.113

To practice producing series graphs, perform the following:

1. With MYSTAT running, open the **Pregnancy** file on the data disk.

   This file contains information about human hormone secretions during a typical pregnancy. Each case number represents a week. Ovulation occurs during the second week and the child's birth occurs at the fortieth week. The three variables are secretions of estrogens (ESTROGEN), pregnanediol (PREGNANE), and chorionic gonadotropin (GONADOTR). The amounts of these hormones secreted during a typical pregnancy change dramatically. The hormone secretion values have been converted to a common scale for easy comparison.

2. Choose the **Series** command under the **Graph** menu to produce the dialog box you see in Figure 3.15.

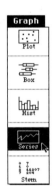

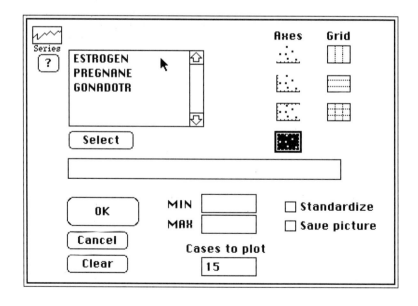

Figure 3.15
Series dialog box

3. Double-click on **ESTROGEN** in the variables box.

4. Type **40** in the "Cases to plot" box so that more than the default fifteen cases are used.
5. Click **OK**.

   You will see the graph in Figure 3.16.

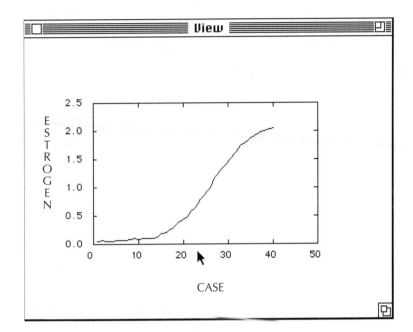

Figure 3.16
Series graph of estrogen secretion during pregnancy

6. Click in the Analysis window, labelled "MYSTAT A Personal version of SYSTAT," to make it active.

In the Analysis window you will also be provided with the following statistics.

Plot of ESTROGEN

Number of cases =   40

Mean of series =   0.778

Standard deviation of series =   0.736

Sequence plot of series

During a normal menstrual cycle, small amounts of estrogen are secreted. When an egg is fertilized and implants in the uterus, the amount of estrogen produced increases. After four to five months, the placental tissues began to produce large amounts of estrogens. The production of estrogen continues to increase until immediately before birth. The series graph clearly shows that this increase does not follow a straight line, but increases dramatically from about the thirteenth week to the thirty-second week and then increases more gradually. Just before birth, the estrogen produced is approximately fifty times that produced in a typical monthly cycle.

■ Proper Graphic Design

Graphs should be designed to present information as accurately and concisely as possible. However, the eye can be easily fooled. To make graphs as *truthful* as possible, a frequently cited rule is to make them as simple as possible while conveying the appropriate message. Interested readers will find *The Elements of Graphing Data* by Cleveland (1985) quite useful for designing proper graphs. Huff (1954) illustrates some techniques to tell lies with graphs. The graphs provided by MYSTAT will seldom give viewers interpretation difficulty when the default options are chosen.

Moving Graphs in the View Window

Sometimes you may need to move a graph to a new position within the View window. For example, when you overlay graphs in the same View window, you can move one graph to the bottom or top of the View window, then use the resizing procedure to direct MYSTAT to draw the next graph in the empty area. Overlaying graphs is discussed in more detail in chapter 8.

To move graphs to new positions, do the following:

1. Make sure the View window is showing. Select **Show window** from the **Goodies** menu if it is not showing.
2. Click in the square into which the graph will be drawn and drag it to a new location within the the View window. Note that the cursor changes to a hand. See Figure 3.17.

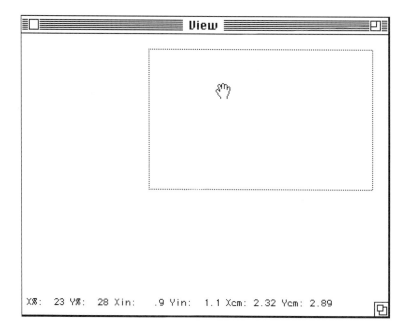

Figure 3.17
Moving the graph

Only the graphs produced using this procedure are drawn in this area.

Resizing Graphs

To see a graph better or to change a graph to a more convenient size, you may need to change the default graph size. MYSTAT's graph resizing capability can potentially improve or degrade the information presented. Figure 3.18 contains two histograms drawn using the same data. In the first graph the variable's scatter appears to be large (the *x*-axis is long) and there doesn't appear to be a great difference in the frequency of any class interval (most of the bars are about the same height). In the second figure, the scatter appears to be small. In this graph the visual differences between frequencies appear to be greater (some of the bars are much taller than others).

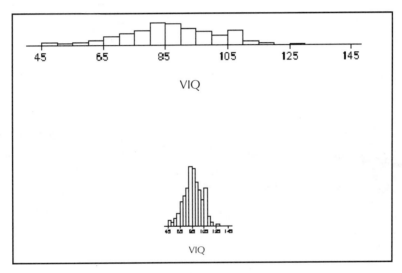

Figure 3.18
Resized histograms of the same data

To change the size of graphs drawn in the View window, use the following steps:

1. If the View window is not showing, select **Show view window** from the **Goodies** menu.
2. Place the cursor in the upper-left corner of the area you want the graph to be drawn in (the cursor should be an arrow, not a hand); then press and drag the cursor to outline the size of the graph you want. Release the button. See Figure 3.19.

All the graphs you produce after these two steps will be placed in this outlined area. You may resize the graph area any number of times. The information at the bottom of the window describes the size of the box in which the graph will be placed. Note that you cannot plot or print a graph that is larger than the View window. If you need a bigger graph, make the View window larger then resize the graph to the appropriate size. When you quit MYSTAT, the default size is again chosen.

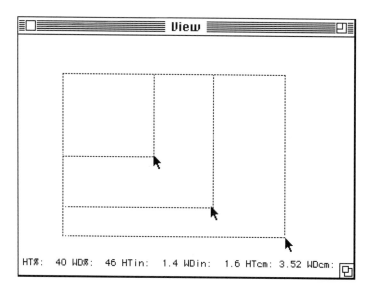

Figure 3.19
Resizing graphs

■ Saving Graphs as PICT Files

Graphs cannot be saved as text files; however, they can be saved as PICT files on a disk. The PICT format is usable by many Macintosh graphics programs. To save the graph check the **Save picture** option in the graph dialog box before clicking **OK** or select the **Save graph as...** command from the **File** menu after you have constructed the graph.

Exercises

1. Produce and optionally print the histogram, stem-and-leaf diagram, and box-and-whiskers plot for the *States* data set on your data disk. The *States* data contains the following five variables: STATE$ (State abbreviation), POPDEN (the population density), SUMMER (the average summer temperature), WINTER (the average winter temperature), and RAIN (the yearly rainfall). Note the distribution shape for each of these variables and whether each distribution is unimodal or has more than one mode. Also note whether the distribution is symmetrical or skewed.

2. Produce box-and-whiskers plots for the numeric variables in the *School Referrals* data using the MDT classification as the grouping variable.

3. Produce and optionally print series graphs for the production of chorionic gonadotropin and pregnanediol using the *Pregnancy* data found on the

data disk. Which one of these two hormones is most similar to estrogen in the way it is produced?

4. There has been considerable concern about the increasing rates of infections from the AIDS virus. In the March–April 1991 issue of *The Courier*, Africa/Caribbean-Pacific-European Community journal, Elizabeth White details the numbers of infections over an eight year period reported to the Caribbean Epidemiology Centre (CAREC). The data are reproduced in the file titled *CAREC Data*. Open this file. The first variable is the reporting year (YEAR) from 1982–1989. The second variable (AID_CASE) is the number of reported cases. Produce a series graph of the number of reported infections. If the graphed trend continues, would you be concerned about the number of reported cases in the future?

5. Also in the same issue of *The Courier*, Simon Horner published data on pages 81-83 detailing the financial assistance given by members of the Development Assistance Committee (DAC). This committee's membership is composed of major countries who have joined together in an attempt to coordinate, adopt, and finance environmental policies which emphasize sustainable development and environmental issues. The file *DAC Data* reproduces part of the report. The first variable (COUNTRY$) names the member countries. The second variable (YEAR88) is the amount of money given by each member country in 1988 in billions of dollars. The third variable (YEAR89) is the number of dollars given in 1989. The fourth variable (GNP89) is the percent of gross national product given in 1989. Using both the 1988 and 1989 figures, are there any countries that can conclude that they are giving enough extra assistance to qualify them as an outside value in a box plot? Which countries, if any are these? The Scandinavian countries appear to be giving higher percentages of their gross national product than others to support sustainable development. Are any of these countries outside values in a box plot?

6. Use the *DAC Data* file, and produce both histograms and stem-and-leaf plots for the three quantitative variables. What are the shapes of these distributions? If the shapes change, why do they do so? If you were either a Japanese or a United States DAC member, would you have a preference about which plot would be used to show how your country supports environmentally sustainable projects in developing countries?

7. In your statistics text there are undoubtedly interesting data sets presented in the beginning chapters. Graph some of these variables and note their shape.

4

Descriptive Statistics

In most statistical textbooks, descriptive statistics is covered in two or three chapters usually called "Measures of Central Tendency," "Measures of Dispersion," or "Characteristics of Distributions." The topics covered are modes, medians, means, ranges, percentiles, quartiles, variances, standard deviations, kurtosis, and skewness. The texts use formulas to calculate measures that describe the characteristics of a variable. For example, *means, medians,* and *modes* describe the most typical value of a variable. *Ranges, quartiles, variances,* and *standard deviations* measure the amount of scatter in a set of data values. Some calculations are conducted on a population or a sample from a population. A *population* is defined as all the objects or subjects that are of interest to the researcher. *Samples* are subsets of populations. Calculations conducted on populations are called *parameters* and are symbolized in textbooks with Greek letters. Examples of population parameters are means (μ), variances (σ^2), and standard deviations (σ). Calculations conducted on samples are called *statistics*. Formulas for these sample statistics are derived so that they are *unbiased estimators* of their respective population parameters. A statistic is an unbiased estimator if, on average its value equals the value of the population parameter. Sample statistics are abbreviated with Roman or English letters. Examples of sample statistics are means ($\overline{X}$), variances (s^2), and standard deviations (s). MYSTAT calculates sample statistics.

Objectives

At the end of this tutorial you should be able to

- Calculate mean, minimum, maximum, sum, standard deviation, variance, skewness, kurtosis, standard error of the mean, and range
- Calculate the statistics above for grouped data
- Use the **Redo last analysis** command
- Print a data set

■ Meanings of the Statistics

Below are brief descriptions of the statistics calculated by MYSTAT and typical formulas for conducting these calculations. Further interpretative information is beyond the scope of this tutorial but can readily be found in any introductory statistics text.

1. **Sum** This is simply found by adding all values together. The Greek symbol Σ simply stands for "add what follows together."

$$\text{sum} = \Sigma X$$

2. **Mean** This is the simple average for the variable. The n stands for the sample size.

$$\overline{X} = \frac{\Sigma X}{n}$$

3. **Minimum** This is the smallest value for the variable.
4. **Maximum** This is the largest value for the variable.
5. **Variance** This is a measure of how scattered the data are.
6. **Standard deviation** This is also a measure of scatter. The standard deviation of a variable is the square root of the variable's variance.
7. **Skew** Skew measures the symmetry of a distribution. Skew was discussed in detail in chapter 3 (see Figure 3.5). A perfectly symmetric distribution has a skew equal to zero. If a distribution is positively skewed, the mean is a larger number than the median, and the skew is appreciably greater than zero. If the mean is a smaller number than the median, the distribution is negatively skewed, and the skew is appreciably less than zero. If a distribution is noticeably skewed, it is called *asymmetric*. In a perfectly symmetric distribution, the mean and median will be equal.
8. **Kurtosis** This is a measure of how *peaked* the distribution is. By definition, normal curves (bell-shaped normal distributions) are considered to be neither peaked or flat; they are called *mesokurtic* and their kurtosis values are close to zero. Distributions that come to a peak faster than normal curves are *leptokurtic* and their kurtosis values are appreciably greater than zero. Distributions that are flatter than normal curves are *platykurtic* and their kurtosis is appreciably less than zero. The term *mesokurtic* must be memorized, but the other terms can be remembered by remembering that you never want to leap off a leptokurtic curve and that a platykurtic curve can be turned over to serve as a plate. Figure 4.1 illustrates these terms.
9. **Standard error of the mean** This is the standard deviation of the sampling distribution of the mean. This statistic is used as a part of the formula for one-sample *t*-tests, which are discussed in chapter 5. The standard error of the mean is calculated using the following formula:

$$s_{\overline{X}} = \frac{s}{\sqrt{n}}$$

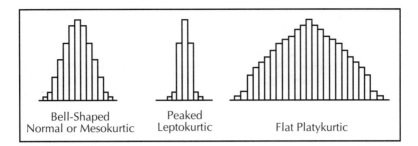

Figure 4.1
Kurtosis of several distributions

10. **Range** This is simply the smallest value recorded subtracted from the largest value recorded. The range gives a very rough indication of the scatter of the scores.

■ Doing the Calculations

Let's calculate descriptive statistics on the Taxpayers' Energy file stored on the data disk. (For an explanation of the variable names see exercise 7 in chapter 2.) After the data is loaded, statistics can be calculated on as many numeric variables as you want. You may also select any combination of statistics available.

The following steps will produce the descriptive statistics using this data set:

1. Open the *Taxpayers' Energy* file on the data disk.
2. Select the **Stats** command under the **Analyze** menu. You will see the dialog box shown in Figure 4.2.

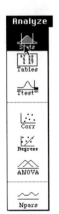

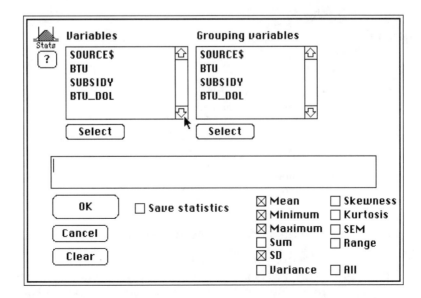

Figure 4.2
Stats dialog box

62 Chapter 4 Descriptive Statistics

If you wanted to calculate statistics on only one variable, you would click on its name once in the "Variables" box and then click once in the **Select** box. When a variable is selected, its name appears in the long rectangular box. If you do not select any variables, MYSTAT will conduct the analysis on every available numeric variable. Since you want to analyze every numeric variable, don't select anything.

If you wanted to do only certain statistics, you would click in the small box next to the statistics wanted. You want to do all the statistics, however, so to select all of them, click in the "All" box.

WARNING: *Some statistics may not be appropriate for all variables.*

3. Click once in the "All" box, and then click **OK**.

   You should produce on your screen the output shown in Table 4.1.

Total observations:	10		
	BTU	SUBSIDY	BTU_DOL
N of cases	10	10	10
Minimum	0.000	0.600	0.000
Maximum	21.000	15.600	12.556
Range	21.000	15.000	12.556
Mean	8.090	4.390	2.799
Variance	73.997	22.043	15.346
Standard dev	8.602	4.695	3.917
Std. error	2.720	1.485	1.239
Skewness	0.510	1.476	1.702
Kurtosis	-1.444	1.254	1.908
Sum	80.900	43.900	27.987

Table 4.1
Output of the Stats command

☞ One problem that students encounter when learning statistics is realizing that statisticians sometimes give different things the same name, sometimes give the same thing different names, and don't always use the same abbreviations. MYSTAT gives us two examples. The standard error of the mean was discussed previously. In the ouput in Table 4.1, MYSTAT titles it Std.error, and in the dialog box (see Figure 4.2) it is abbreviated SEM. For standard deviations, texts often use the abbreviation S. The MYSTAT dialog box labels standard deviations SD, and the output abbreviates standard deviations standard dev.

Using Redo Last Analysis

Suppose you needed to submit a paper copy of these results for class credit. When you begin conducting statistical analyses, mistakes are frequent companions. You may enter a wrong value into the worksheet or fill out a dialog box incorrectly. If you do an analysis of the wrong data or give the computer the wrong set of directions, the output will be incorrect. If you are printing your results, you do not want to print the mistakes. Usually it is good form to conduct the analyses, and then send the results to the window to check your results. Remember you can enlarge the screen to see more of your results at one time. Also if the results rush by too quickly to see during the output, you can scroll back in the Analysis window to see all of your results as described in chapter 3. Once you have exactly what you want, then **Results to printer** and **Redo last analysis** become quick and convenient procedures for sending the perfected results to the printer without reentering all the needed information into the dialog box for the analysis. If a printer is attached to your computer you will receive several dialog boxes that you must fill out to direct the output to the correct printer. Usually just clicking the **OK** box(es) will fulfill your duty. If you have any questions, ask your instructor.

To print your analysis after checking it on screen, follow these steps:

☞ If you are not printing your results, omit step 1 below.

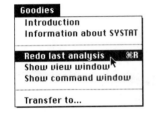

1. Choose **Results to printer** under the **Data** menu.
2. Choose **Redo last analysis** under the **Goodies** menu. (Alternatively, you could choose the **Stats** command under the **Analyze** menu again. If you do so, you will need to fill out the dialog box again.)

The descriptive statistics calculated on the Taxpayers' Energy data are calculated again, and Table 4.1 will be printed.

■ Calculating Statistics for Grouped Data

In data sets, you often have subgroups that are of interest, and you may want to calculate separate descriptive statistics for each group. For MYSTAT to calculate descriptive statistics for groups within a data set, the file must be sorted according to the grouping variables. For example, in the *School Referrals* file, the MDT variable defines the group each child was assigned to. (See chapter 2, "Reading a Text File" for additional information concerning this data set.) Suppose we want to compare the verbal IQ and performance IQ of each group.

To begin the process you will need to sort the *School Referrals* file. Follow these steps:

1. Open the *School Referrals* data set.
2. Select **Sort** under the **Data** menu.
3. When the dialog box appears, double-click on **MDT** in the "Select sort variables" box. (For further information on the **Sort** command, see chapter 2.) Then click **OK**.

Chapter 4 Descriptive Statistics

4. A second dialog box will appear asking if MYSTAT can save the sorted file with the title *School Referrals Sorted*. To allow this to happen, click once in the **Save** button.

   ☞ If you want to use some other name, type in that name and then click once on the **Save** button.

You have just produced and saved a file in which all the cases are sorted (ordered) on the variable MDT. All the children who were assigned to group 1 are first in the file, all the children who were assigned to group 2 are next, and so on.

The following steps will produce separate descriptive statistics for each of the MDT groups:

1. Open the file **School Referrals Sorted**.
2. Select **Stats** from the **Analyze** menu.
3. Select **VIQ** and **PIQ** in the "Variables" box by double-clicking on both.
4. Double-click on **MDT** in the "Grouping variables" box.

   Note that *VIQ PIQ*MDT* appears in the dialog box window.
5. Click the **All** option to clear the settings. Then choose the Mean, Variance, Standard Deviation, Skewness, and Kurtosis for these statistics by clicking in the appropriate box to turn that calculation option on.
6. Click **OK**.

   All the descriptive statistics selected in step 5 for the variables VIQ and PIQ will be calculated separately for every group defined by the MDT variable.

☞ If the output is too long to be visible in the Analysis window, you can enlarge this window or scroll back to see the earlier results. However, the Analysis window can only handle so much information even if the "Scroll analyses" box has been checked in the **Formats** dialog box (see chapter 2, Figure 2.28). If the output is quite long, you will overrun the capacity of the Analysis window to store the output. If you did not follow the procedures above, the output for this analysis is very likely to be too long for the Analysis window.

The following seven tables are representative of the entire analysis. You should now be able to scroll throughout your screen. You should see the output shown in Table 4.2.

Table 4.2a

The following results are for:		
MDT =		1.000
Total observations:	20	
	VIQ	PIQ
N of cases	20	20
Mean	64.700	69.450
Variance	126.221	136.787
Standard dev	11.235	11.696
Skewness	-0.117	-0.584
Kurtosis	-0.632	-0.366

Table 4.2b

The following results are for:		
MDT =		2.000
Total observations:	20	
	VIQ	PIQ
N of cases	20	20
Mean	98.000	94.700
Variance	60.211	131.379
Standard dev	7.760	11.462
Skewness	0.264	0.324
Kurtosis	-0.566	-1.021

Table 4.2c

The following results are for:		
MDT =		3.000
Total observations:	138	
	VIQ	PIQ
N of cases	138	138
Mean	84.862	90.507
Variance	125.390	166.164
Standard dev	11.198	12.890
Skewness	0.106	-0.113
Kurtosis	-0.086	-0.006

Table 4.2d

The following results are for:		
MDT =		4.000
Total observations:		8
	VIQ	PIQ
N of cases	8	8
Mean	102.125	102.250
Variance	57.268	78.500
Standard dev	7.568	8.860
Skewness	-0.317	-0.502
Kurtosis	-0.967	-0.912

Table 4.2e

The following results are for:		
MDT =		5.000
Total observations:		2
	VIQ	PIQ
N of cases	2	2
Mean	66.000	88.000
Variance	32.000	18.000
Standard dev	5.657	4.243
Skewness	0.000	0.000
Kurtosis	-2.000	-2.000

Table 4.2f

The following results are for:		
MDT =		6.000
Total observations:		11
	VIQ	PIQ
N of cases	11	11
Mean	110.091	115.000
Variance	39.091	136.400
Standard dev	6.252	11.679
Skewness	1.160	0.256
Kurtosis	0.995	-0.973

The following results are for:
MDT   =   7.000

Total observations: 1

	VIQ	PIQ
N of cases	1	1
Mean	46.000	54.000
Variance	0.000	0.000
Standard dev	0.000	0.000
Skewness	0.000	0.000
Kurtosis	0.000	0.000

Table 4.2g Descriptive statistics output for the School Referrals file sorted on MDT

Notice that there are separate outputs for the seven different groups within this data set. Look at group 1's output. Their mean IQs are reported as 64.700 and 69.450. Both these scores are within the range for defining a youngster as educable mentally retarded. The children in group 4 had average IQs. These youngsters were not placed in a special educational program. Group 7 contains a single child, so the scatter and shape statistics cannot be calculated. From this analysis, we can see that the groups assigned by the MDT differed dramatically in both VIQ and PIQ. If every value for a variable is the same, which of the descriptive statistics calculated by MYSTAT would have values of zero?

■ Printing Data Sets

It is often easier to edit data files if they can be printed on paper rather than sent to the computer screen. Selecting **Results to printer** only prints analyses and graphs. In chapter 2, I mentioned that there is a method for printing data sets not mentioned in any of the MYSTAT manuals. The command **Print selected text...** under the **File** menu enables you to send output *previously* sent to the Analysis window to the printer. The trick is to get the data copied from the Data Editor window to the Analysis window so that it can be selected and sent to the printer. Here are the steps.

> **WARNING:** *These steps only work for relatively small data sets. If the data set is large, you will need to repeat these steps to print small sections of the file.*

1. Open the **Taxpayers' Energy** file.
2. Make sure that the Data Editor window and the Analysis window are open.

   If the Analysis window is not open, an easy way to create one is to do some descriptive statistics on a single variable. Remember all statistical output goes to the Analysis window, so MYSTAT will need to open this window to display the output.
3. Make the Data Editor window active by clicking in it.

4. Use the **Select all** command under the **Edit** menu. You should see all the cells in the Data Editor window darken to indicate that they have been selected.
5. Choose **Copy** from the **Edit** menu.
6. Click in the Analysis window (statistics output window) to make it active.
7. Use the **Paste** command from the **Edit** menu. All your data should be pasted into the Analysis window (see Figure 4.3).
8. Drag the cursor through all the data you wish to select, in this case, all of it.
9. Choose the **Print selected text** command from the **File** menu.

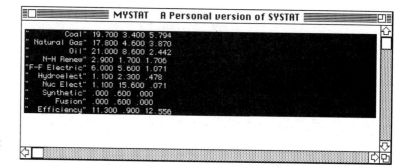

Figure 4.3
The Analysis window before choosing **Print selected text**

That's all there is to it. If the data set is very long, you will need to repeat this procedure for parts of the data set so that you don't overflow the Analysis. Note in your printed output that the data does not necessarily line up in neat columns as it does in the Data Editor.

Exercises

1. For the data stored in the files *Cities*, *States*, *School Referrals*, and *DAC Data*, calculate and optionally print all available descriptive statistics for every quantitative variable. Decide if the variables are symmetrical or skewed. If they are skewed, are they positively or negatively skewed? Describe the kurtosis of each variable. Are the variables mesokurtic, leptokurtic or platykurtic? Which measure of central tendency (mean, median, or mode) would be the best to describe each variable?

2. For both the *States* and *Cities* files, you have previously produced stem-and-leaf and box plots. Compare Hspread values and standard deviations using these files. Write a sentence or two describing the relationships, if any, that you found between these statistics.

5

One-Sample Statistical Tests

There are two types of statistics: descriptive and inferential. Up to this point, you have been producing and interpreting descriptive statistics, which are calculated to disclose some characteristic of a sample data set. You have produced measures that indicate typical scores in the distribution (mean, median, and mode), measures of scatter (range, variance, standard deviation), measures of shape (skew and kurtosis), and visualizations of the data values (histograms, stem-and-leaf plots, box plots).

Inferential statistics are produced to make estimates of population parameters and to make decisions concerning those parameters. The first inferential tests taught in most introductory statistical texts are the one-sample z-test and the one-sample t-test. You use these tests when you want to determine whether a mean is statistically different than the mean of a known or hypothesized population.

Objectives

At the end of this tutorial you should be able to

- Determine if you should conduct a one sample z-test or a one sample t-test
- Know how to use the ZCF and ZIF functions within the Data Editor
- Calculate and interpret one-sample z-tests
- Calculate and interpret one-sample t-tests

Determining Whether the One-sample z- or t-Test Is Appropriate

Both one-sample z- and t-tests are used when the researcher wants to decide if a sample mean is different from a known or hypothesized population mean. If you know the population standard deviation (σ), the most appropriate test is the one-sample z-test. If you do not know the population standard deviation, choose the one-sample t-test. Figure 5.1 illustrates a decision model that will be expanded in future chapters. The diamonds represent questions, the arrows represent the answers to those questions, and the rectangles depict the decision. Circles are connecting symbols directing you to start or stop or to go to another decision diagram in a specific chapter. For example, the circle with the 6 inside it in Figure 5.1 directs you to go to the decision diagram in chapter 6.

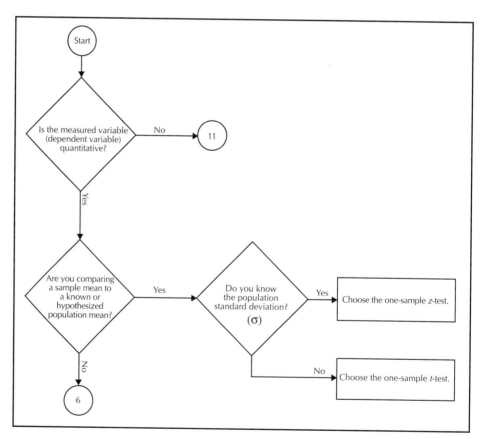

Figure 5.1
Decision model for one-sample z- or t-test

If you are conducting a one-sample z-test, one of the things you want to know is if the mean of the sample is significantly different from the population mean. To test for significant differences, statisticians set up null and alternative hypotheses. The *null hypothesis* is a hypothesis used in statistical testing that specifies a specific value for the population parameter. The *alternative* hypothesis is a hypothesis that states that the population parameter is something other than that specified by the null hypothesis. These hypotheses can either take directional (one-tailed) or nondirectional (two-tailed) forms. In a *directional* problem, the alternative hypothesis states that the parameter is either greater than or less than some specified value. A *nondirectional* problem's alternative hypothesis simply specifies that the population parameter is not equal to some specific value. The null and alternative hypotheses are always mutually exclusive; that is, if one is true, the other must be false. The null and alternative hypotheses are usually stated in the form of an equation.

Statistical analysis involves hypothesis testing. On the basis of your data analysis, using the appropriate statistical test, you will decide whether or not you reject or fail to reject the null hypothesis. If you reject a null hypothesis that is correct, you have made an error. This error is called a *Type 1 error*, and it is determined by setting the *alpha (α) level* or *probability* for an experiment. To decide on the alpha level, you must consider how often you will tolerate making a Type 1 error. Setting an alpha level of 0.05 means that there is a five percent probability that a Type 1 error will occur, or that you will tolerate being wrong when you reject the null hypothesis five percent of the time. While you may choose any alpha, alpha levels of .05, .01 and .001 have been traditionally used by statisticians. Which of these alpha levels you chose depends upon the experimental situation. The smaller the alpha level, the less often you make a Type 1 error, but a small alpha also makes rejecting the null hypothesis more difficult.

Once you have set the alpha level for a *z*-test, you need to determine the critical *z* value that marks the boundary for rejecting the null hypothesis. The *critical value* is the *z* score, which yields the chosen alpha level in a normal distribution. If your *z* value is outside the critical value, you reject the null hypothesis; otherwise, you fail to reject it.

Figure 5.2 illustrates that 5% (.05) or fewer *z* scores are found below the value of –1.645. The same can be said for a *z* value of +1.645. For two-tailed tests, 5% of the *z* values (each tail has 2½%) are outside the values of ±1.96. If the obtained *z* value was beyond 1.645 for a one-tailed test, or beyond ±1.96 for a two-tailed test, the null hypothesis is rejected. Critical *z* values are usually found in a table in the appendix of most statistics texts. With MYSTAT, you don't need the table. MYSTAT's ZIF function finds critical *z* values from alpha levels, and MYSTAT's ZCF function finds the alpha level from observed *z* values.

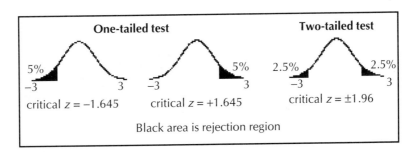

Figure 5.2
Critical *z* values at alpha = .05

ZIF

If you enter the alpha level for the experiment into the Data Editor window, MYSTAT will calculate the associated z value using the ZIF function.

To use the ZIF function to find several critical z values do the following:

1. Select **New** under the **File** menu.

    This will clear the Data Editor window and allow you to enter new data.

2. Click once on the Data Editor window to make certain it is active and ready to receive data.

3. Type **ALPHA** to name the variable for which you want to enter alpha values.

4. Type **CRIT_Z** to name the variable for which the critical z values will be computed using the ZIF function.

5. Type in the alpha values of **.001, .010, .025, .050,** and **.10**.

    ☞ You can enter these values down by typing the value and then pressing the down arrow key instead of [Return].

The Data Editor window should look like Figure 5.3.

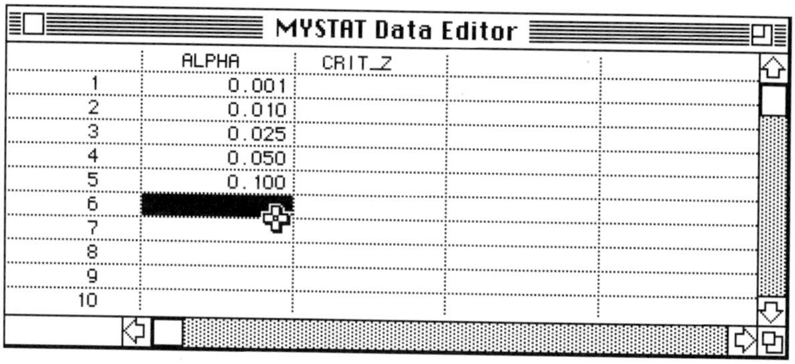

Figure 5.3
The Data Editor window prepared for the ZIF function

	ALPHA	CRIT_Z
1	0.001	
2	0.010	
3	0.025	
4	0.050	
5	0.100	
6		
7		
8		
9		
10		

6. Select the **Math...** command under the **Editor** menu.

    You will fill out the dialog box so that the variable CRIT_Z is calculated using the ZIF function on ALPHA. Before clicking **OK**, the dialog box should look like Figure 5.4.

7. Select **CRIT-Z** in the "Variables" box. It will appear in the "Set Variable" box.

8. Select **ZIF ( )** in the "Functions" box. It will appear in the " to Variable or expression" box.

    ☞ You will need to use the scroll bar in the dialog box's "Functions" box to get to ZIF ( ).

Determining Whether the One-Sample z- or t-Test Is Appropriate

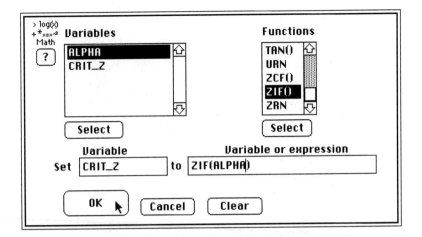

Figure 5.4
The completed dialog box

9. Select **Alpha** from the "Variables" box. It will appear in parentheses next to **ZIF** in the "to Variable or expression" box.

10. Click **OK**.

MYSTAT will calculate the critical z values found in Figure 5.5.

	ALPHA	CRIT_Z
1	.001	-3.090
2	.010	-2.326
3	.025	-1.960
4	.050	-1.645
5	.100	-1.282

Figure 5.5
Critical z values from the ZIF function

You have just created a table of critical z values. Compare the values shown in Figure 5.5 to the ones in your textbook. MYSTAT does the job quickly and can report values that are not contained in the tables because of lack of space. If you want to, save these values as *Critical z*.

ZCF

The ZCF function is the reverse of the ZIF function. Using MYSTAT and the ZCF function (*z* score cumulative function) you can find the alpha level of any observed *z* value.

74 Chapter 5 One-Sample Statistical Tests

Here is how to do it. After you have calculated a *z* value,

1. Under the **File** menu choose **New**.
2. Type **Z** to name the obtained *z* value.
3. Type **ALPHA** for the second variable name.
4. Type **2.9457** for the obtained *z* value.

☞ The Data Editor will display 2.946 because of the default format.

Your Data Editor should look like Figure 5.6.

Figure 5.6
Data Editor with a *z* score

5. Use the **Math** command under the **Editor** menu to calculate the value of ZCF(Z) for ALPHA.
6. Fill in the dialog box so that it looks like Figure 5.7.

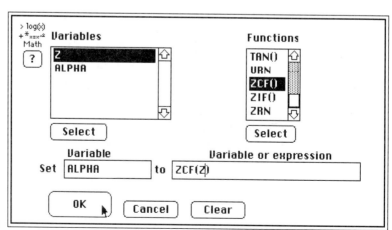

Figure 5.7
The **Math...** dialog box

7. Click **OK**.

The alpha level will be calculated and the Data Editor window will look like Figure 5.8.

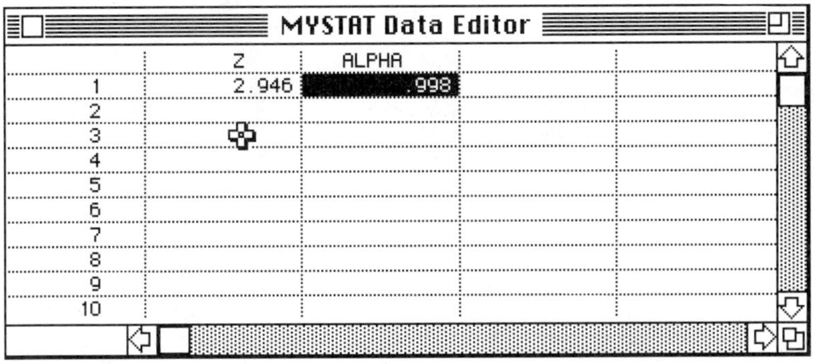

Figure 5.8
Alpha level from the ZCF function

The alpha calculated is .998. This is the area under a normal curve below a z score of 2.9457, or the probability of obtaining a z value equal to or below 2.9457. In Figure 5.7, it is the darkened area under the curve. To create the alpha value for a one-tailed z-test, create another variable where you subtract .998 from 1.0. To create the alpha level for a two-tailed z-test, you multiply the one-tailed alpha value by 2. You do not need to save the values you just calculated.

These tables are often found in statistics books. You will find just such a data set on your data disk titled *Z values*. Open it up at your leisure and compare the values found there to the values in your statistics text.

■ One-Sample *z*-Test

As noted in Figure 5.1, the one-sample z-test is used when you know the population mean (μ) and the population standard deviation (σ) and you wish to compare a sample mean ($\overline{X}$) to the population mean to see if the sample mean is reliably different from the population mean. A z statistic is normally distributed. This tutorial will demonstrate how MYSTAT can be used to help do the z-test.

The Problem

Suppose that you are a third grade reading teacher. You know the third grade population on average earns a score of 100 with a standard deviation of 15 on a popular reading test. You have decided to introduce a new reading series into your class this year. You wonder if this reading program will change the reading scores. At the end of the academic year you give your students the reading test. Their scores have been entered in the MYSTAT data file titled *Reading*. When you open this file, note that there are thirty students in this sample. The data are reproduced for you in Table 5.1.

NAME$	READING
Betty B.	100.000
Bob H.	98.000
Claudia W.	89.000
Donald D.	88.000
Donald W.	97.000

Table 5.1 cont.

NAME$	READING
Douglas A.	111.000
Dwayne W.	104.000
Eric L.	92.000
Hays D.	134.000
Heidi H.	106.000
Janet T.	99.000
Jean R.	108.000
Jill B.	103.000
John V.	91.000
Judy S.	112.000
Kevin T.	117.000
Lance R.	129.000
Lesley S.	122.000
Linda C.	132.000
Linda G.	107.000
Lisa S.	130.000
Melvin S.	90.000
Michael A.	111.000
Nichole B.	99.000
Pam M.	109.000
Regie T.	118.000
Stanley Q.	120.000
Stephanie D.	102.000
Todd A.	102.000
Todd K.	122.000

Table 5.1
The data from the *Reading* file

The Solution

Almost all inferential statistical problems can be broken down into six distinct steps. Of these steps, only the third and fourth steps require using the computer. All the others require you to use your head. We'll use the six-step solution to conduct a one-sample *z*-test.

1. Write the null and alternative hypotheses.

Before you can write the null and alternative hypotheses, you must decide whether you have a directional (one-tailed) or nondirectional (two-tailed) problem. Here the teacher is interested in whether her reading program changes the children's reading scores, so this is a nondirectional (two-tailed) test. The null and alternative hypotheses are

$H_0: \mu = 100$
$H_1: \mu \neq 100$

2. Set the alpha level.

Remember, the alpha level determines how often you will tolerate making a Type 1 error, and a Type 1 error occurs when you reject the null hypothesis when it is true. The common alpha level of .05 ($\alpha = .05$) is fine for this example.

3. Collect the data and enter it into MYSTAT.

1. Open the *Reading* file on the data disk.

4. Calculate the statistic.

In this case it is the one-sample *z* statistic whose formula is

$$Z = \frac{\overline{X} - \mu}{\sigma_{\overline{X}}}$$

μ is the symbol for the *population mean*. Its value is the same as the known or hypothesized mean given in the problem. In this example, the value is 100. The standard deviation of the sampling distribution of the mean is called the *standard error of the mean* and is symbolized by $\sigma_{\overline{X}}$. The value of the standard error of the mean is given by the population standard deviation (σ) divided by the square root of the sample size (n). The formula for the standard error of the mean is

$$\sigma_{\overline{X}} = \frac{\sigma}{\sqrt{n}} = \frac{15}{\sqrt{30}} = 2.7386.$$

The only part of the calculation not found directly from the information in the problem is the sample mean, $\overline{X}$. This can be easily found using the computer.

Do the following four steps using MYSTAT:

1. Select the **Stats** command under the **Analyze** menu.
2. Select the READING variable by double-clicking on it in the "Variables" box.
3. Choose the Mean as the statistic you want to calculate.
4. Click **OK**.

    MYSTAT calculates the mean, which is 108.067. Fitting everything into the equation for the one-sample *z*-test gives an obtained value of

    $$Z = \frac{108.067 - 100}{2.7386} = 2.9457.$$

5. Decide whether or not to reject the null hypothesis.

You must either reject or fail to reject the null hypothesis. For z-tests, this decision can be made in two ways. The first is to compare your obtained z value with a critical z value. If your obtained z value is outside of the critical z value, then you reject the null hypothesis. The critical z values for a two-tailed test where α = .05 are ±1.96. Your obtained value of 2.9457 is outside ±1.96, so you reject the null hypothesis.

The second method will give the same results. Using the second method, you compare the probability of your obtained z value with the alpha level you set for the experiment. If the probability of your obtained z value is less than the alpha level, you reject the null hypothesis. The probability of a z equal to 2.9457 is .004. We know this because we calculated this using the ZCF function. Because .004 is less than the alpha of .05, you reject the null hypothesis.

☞ Further information concerning this step is found in the section, "Using ZCF and ZIF."

6. Make a summary statement about the statistical analysis.

In this case you might say something like, "The teacher found that after introducing her new reading procedure, the students' scores significantly increased (Z = 2.946, p < .05)."

■ One-Sample *t*-Test

As noted in Figure 5.1, a one-sample *t*-test is used when a sample mean is to be compared to a known or hypothesized population mean, and the standard deviation of the population is unknown. Since it is likely that we will *not* know the population standard deviation, one-sample *t*-tests are used far more frequently than one-sample z-tests. MYSTAT does not have a specific procedure for one-sample *t*-tests but as with the z-test, we can work around this and have MYSTAT help us do the calculation.

The Problem You are a biomedical researcher and you want to know if the consumption of alcohol during pregnancy affects the birth weight of babies. You know that the average birth weight for babies in the United States is 7 lbs., 10 oz. This converts to 7.625 lbs., and is the population mean (μ). You draw a random sample from hospital records of the birth weights of infants whose mothers indicated that they regularly consumed alcohol during pregnancy. The birth weights have been entered in the MYSTAT data file *Birth weight*. Because you do not know the variance or standard deviation of the population, this type of problem is solved using the one-sample *t*-test instead of the one-sample z-test.

The Solution Apply the six-step solution.

1. Write the null and alternative hypotheses.

Because you only want to know if birth weights are changed, this is a two-tailed test. If you wanted to find out whether or not alcohol consumption decreased birth weight, this would be a one-tailed test.

H_0: $\mu = 7.625$

H_1: $\mu \neq 7.625$ lbs.

2. Set the alpha level.

Again select $\alpha = .05$.

3. Collect the data and enter it into MYSTAT.

The data are already stored for you in the *Birth weight* file. When you open this file note that there are thirty-two cases. The variables are the child's first name, NAME$, its birth weight in pounds, WEIGHT, and its sex, SEX$.

4. Calculate the statistic.

You want to calculate the one-sample *t* statistic. To do this you need to tell MYSTAT what the population mean (μ) is. You will need to create a new variable called POP_MEAN for this data set.

1. Scroll to the top of the data set, and type **POP_MEAN** to name your new variable.

    The hypothesized population mean is 7.625. This is the value that you are going to use for POP_MEAN for every case. This is easy using the **Math...** command under the **Editor** menu.

2. Select **Math** from the **Editor** menu, and fill out the dialog box so that it looks like Figure 5.9.

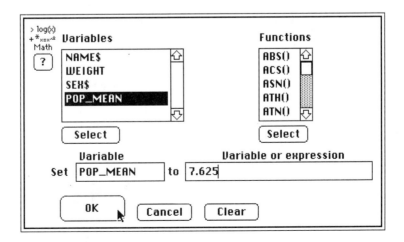

Figure 5.9
The completed **Math...** dialog box

3. Click **OK** to set POP_MEAN to 7.625 for every case. Your data should look like Figure 5.10.

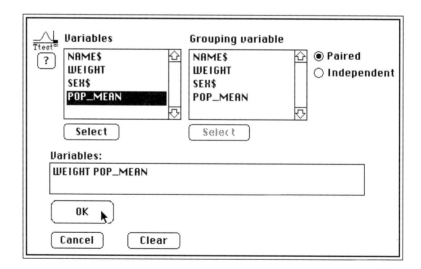

Figure 5.10
The *Birth weight* data set

4. To calculate the *t*-test, select the **Ttest** command under the **Analyze** menu.
5. Select **Weight** and **Pop_Mean** in the "Variables" box. Note that the option for Paired test is chosen. The dialog box should look like Figure 5.11.

Figure 5.11
Completed **Ttest** dialog box

6. Click **OK**.

The results shown in Table 5.2 should appear.

Table 5.2
Results from completed *t*-test

Paired Samples t-test on WEIGHT vs POP_MEAN with 32 cases.

Mean difference = -1.269
SD difference   =   1.288
DF   =   31
T   =   5.573
Prob =   0.000

These results include a heading or title that indicates the type of *t*-test conducted and the names of the variables used in the calculation. The mean difference between the variable values and the population mean is reported followed by the standard deviation (SD) of that difference. The *degrees of freedom* (DF) are then reported. Degrees of freedom are the number of values in the sample data that are free to vary given that you know the value for the statistic. The *t* value is then reported followed by the significance or probability of obtaining a *t* statistic whose absolute value is as large or larger by chance.

5. Decide whether or not to reject the the null hypothesis.

To make this decision for *t*-tests, you look at the probability associated with the *t* value. If the probability of that *t* value occurring by chance is less than the alpha level, then you reject the null hypothesis. Otherwise you fail to reject the null hypothesis. In this case, the probability is 0.000 which is less than the alpha level of .05. Therefore, we obviously reject the null hypothesis that these babies came from a population of infants whose birth weights averaged 7.625 pounds.

WARNING: *If the probability value is less than 0.0005, MYSTAT simply reports that the Prob = 0.000. Statisticians never report that a probability equals 0.000 in a summary statement. You should report zero values as probabilities less than 0.0005.*

6. Make a summary statement about the statistical analysis.

In this case, you might write "The average birth weight of infants whose mothers consumed alcohol while pregnant (6.356 lbs.) was significantly lower than the national average (7.625 lbs.) (t = 5.573, df = 31, p < 0.0005)."

Note that the heading provided for the output of the *t*-test is not appropriate. This was not a paired samples *t*-test but a one-sample *t*-test. The output in the Analysis window should be changed:

1. Click in the Analysis window to make it active.
2. Click the cursor ahead of the words *Paired Samples*, hold the mouse button down and drag through these words. The Analysis window will look like Figure 5.12.

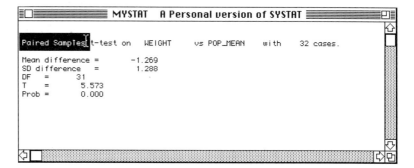

Figure 5.12
The Analysis window with **Paired Samples** highlighted

3. Type the words **One-sample**; this will replace *Paired samples*.

   To print the analysis with the corrected heading, you need to choose **Print selected text** rather than **Results to printer**.

4. Select the **All** command under the **Edit** menu. All of the text should be highlighted.

5. Choose **Print selected text** from the **File** menu.

   Your final output should look like Table 5.3.

One-sample t-test on WEIGHT vs POP_MEAN with 32 cases.

Mean difference =   -1.269
SD difference   =   1.288
DF   =   31
T   =   5.573
Prob =   0.000

Table 5.3
Corrected *t*-test output

☞ You may want to type the value of the population mean (7.625 lbs. in this example) into the Analysis window to further document the output.

Exercises

1. It is known that for a population of joggers the mean time required to run one mile is 10.2 minutes with a standard deviation of 1.16 minutes. A sample of joggers is given a special fitness training program and then tested on the time they take to finish a one-mile run. The data are found in the file *Joggers*. Did the fitness program significantly affect the joggers' time? Write the null and alternative hypotheses along with your summary statement.

2. It is hypothesized that the drug tamoxifan significantly increases the survival time of women who have been diagnosed as having a certain type of aggressive breast cancer. It is also known that on average women with this cancer live only 2.75 years after diagnosis. The Women's Cancer Center has given a random sample of patients tamoxifan and notes their survival rates over a five-year span. State the null and alternative hypotheses. The data are contained in the data set titled *Cancer*. Did tamoxifan increase these women's survival time? Write the null and alternative hypotheses along with your summary statement.

3. Use the *States* data set. Determine whether the average rainfall in the United States in the year surveyed was 20 inches. Write the null and alternative hypotheses along with your summary statement.

4. Answer any assigned problems from your text using MYSTAT. Write the null and alternative hypotheses along with your summary statement.

6

Two-Sample Statistical Tests

Sometimes you will need to compare the means of two samples to determine whether they are different. If a treatment is given to one sample and not to the other and the means of the samples are different, the treatment may have produced this difference. In this chapter, we investigate differences between the means of two samples. This is the classic application of the *t*-test.

Two *t*-tests will be discussed in this chapter: the *independent t-test* and the *dependent t-test*. In some texts the independent *t*-test is called the two-sample *t*-test. The dependent *t* might be called the paired or correlated *t*-test. The dependent *t*-test also may be called a two-sample test when subjects are matched on an important variable like age or weight.

Objectives

At the end of this tutorial you will be able to
- Differentiate when to use a dependent or independent *t*-test
- Use MYSTAT to calculate the dependent and independent *t* values
- Interpret *t*-test results
- Know the assumptions underlying these tests

Independent Versus Dependent *t*-test

Both the independent and dependent *t*-tests are used to decide whether or not two sample means are different from each other. If the two samples are not related to each other, conduct an independent *t*-test. If there is a relationship between the two samples, use the dependent *t*-test. Figure 6.1 illustrates this decision model. Remember that circles are connecting symbols directing you to start or stop or go to another decision diagram in a specific chapter. For example, the circle with the 5 inside it tells you that this decision diagram continues from chapter 5.

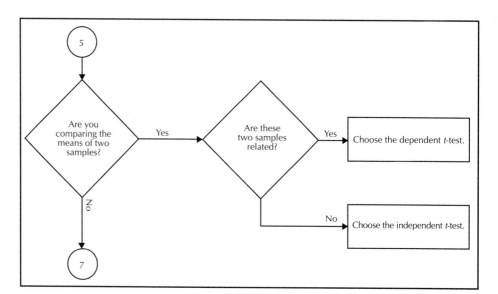

Figure 6.1
Decision model for independent or dependent *t*-test

Independent *t*-Test

As noted in Figure 6.1, the *independent t-test* is used when the two samples are unrelated (the people in the first sample are unrelated to the people in the second sample). This is the case when subjects are randomly assigned to an experimental group or a control group. We will illustrate a problem using MYSTAT and the six-step solution.

The Problem

You are the project director for a pharmaceutical company that is marketing a new drug for the treatment of the HIV virus. You have gone through the toxicology tests and you are now working on an experiment with monkeys. You randomly select and assign fifty subjects that are HIV positive to two different groups. The control group gets a pill with no active ingredients (a placebo). The treatment group receives your drug. To test the effectiveness of the drug, your company has devised a sophisticated method to measure the degree to which a monkey's immune system has been compromised. The numbers run from zero (no compromise) to 100 (the immune system is fully compromised). After one year both groups are examined and their immune system scores are tabulated. You want to see whether or not the two groups' immune systems have responded differently.

The Solution

Below is the six-step solution.

1. Write the null and alternative hypotheses.

The null hypothesis is that there are no differences between the two samples. If the null hypothesis is true, then the two samples come from populations that have identical means (the population parameters are identical).

$H_o: \mu1 = \mu2$

$H_1: \mu1 \neq \mu2$

2. Set the alpha level.

For this experiment set the α level to .05.

3. Collect the data and enter it into MYSTAT.

These data are provided in the file *AIDS*. Note when you open this file that there is a variable labeled GROUP. This is the group to which each subject was assigned. (The subjects given the number 1 are in the control group; the subjects given the number 2 are in the experimental group.) The next variable, IMSCORE, is the subject's immune system score. Scroll through the data. There are twenty-five group 1 subjects and twenty-five group 2 subjects. Are there differences between the two groups that are readily apparent?

4. Calculate the statistic.

1. Select **Ttest** under the **Analyze** menu.
2. Make sure that the **Independent** option is chosen. This option is in the upper right-hand corner of the dialog box. This directs MYSTAT to do an independent *t*-test.
3. Double-click on **IMSCORE** in the "Variables" box. IMSCORE is the dependent variable in the analysis. The dependent variable is the variable that is measured in the experiment and the one whose mean is compared across the two sample groups.
4. Double-click on **GROUP** in the "Grouping variable" box. The GROUP variable indicates to which of the two sample groups the dependent variable (IMSCORE) belongs. The dialog box should look like Figure 6.2. The asterisk before GROUP indicates that GROUP is the grouping variable.

WARNING: *If you attempt to select a variable in the "Grouping variable" box that is not coded with a 1 or a 2, you will get an error message because independent t-tests only are appropriate for two groups.*

Figure 6.2
Ttest dialog box for independent t-test

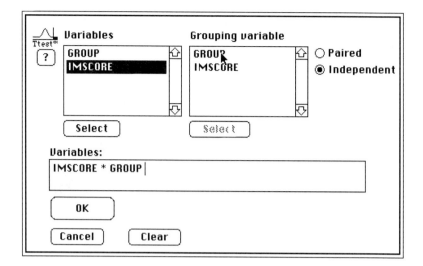

5. Click **OK**.

The results of this analysis are presented in Table 6.1.

Table 6.1
Independent t-test results

Independent samples t-test on IMSCORE grouped by GROUP

Group	N	Mean	SD
1.000	25	32.760	21.008
2.000	25	18.240	10.760

Separate variances	t = 3.076	df = 35.8	prob = .004
Pooled variances	t = 3.076	df = 48	prob = .003

We assume that not only are µ1 and µ2 equal (see the null hypothesis in step 1 of the six-step solution) but that the variances of the two populations are equal. To estimate that common variance, we combine (or pool) the variances from both samples, and MYSTAT reports this as a *pooled variance*. Both a separate variances and a pooled variances *t* value are reported. The separate variances *t* value uses the separate variances within each group for its calculation. If variances differ substantially, use the separate variances *t* value. See exercise 2 at the end of this chapter for practice on this.

The degrees of freedom (df) for this problem are also reported. Remember that degrees of freedom were defined in chapter 5 as the number of values in the sample data that are free to vary given that the value for the descriptive statistic is known. The separate variances degrees of freedom are calculated differently; they decrease as the variances become more different. MYSTAT always provides the degrees of freedom when it conducts a statistical test that uses them.

The designations group 1 and group 2 are not very meaningful. You can change the output in the Analysis window by typing in the name of the group. You might change the output for this analysis to look like Table 6.2. For detailed directions about changing the output in the Analysis window see chapter 5 and the discussion concerning the one-sample *t*-test.

Table 6.2 Corrected independent *t*-test output

Independent samples t-test on IMSCORE grouped by GROUP

Group	N	Mean	SD
Control	25	32.760	21.008
Treatment	25	18.240	10.760

Separate variances	t = 3.076	df = 35.8	prob = .004
Pooled variances	t = 3.076	df = 48	prob = .003

Note that the symbol MYSTAT uses to report independent *t* value is a lower case *t*.

5. Decide whether or not to reject the null hypothesis.

The probability of .003 is smaller than the alpha level of .05 set in step 2; therefore, you reject the null hypothesis.

☞ The decision making process for rejecting the null hypothesis when using the *t*-test is the same as that used for the *z*-test. If the probability is less than the alpha level, reject the null hypothesis.

6. Write a summary statement.

Since you rejected the null hypothesis, the summary statement might go something like this: "There was a significant difference between the immune system scores for the subjects who took the new drug when compared to those who received no treatment. Subjects in the treatment group had immune systems that were less compromised than those in the control group, (t = 3.076, df = 48, p = .003, two-tailed).

■ Dependent *t*-Test

The *dependent t-test* is used when the subjects in the experiment are measured twice or matched on one or more attributes. Dependent *t*-tests can be used for both one and two-sample situations. The same statistical formula is used for both.

Two-Sample Situation

The dependent *t*-test is used with two separate groups when the cases or subjects are matched. This typically happens when the investigator matches subjects (makes sure they are the same in some way) and randomly assigns one member of the matched pair to the experimental group and the other member to the control group. This design frequently is employed in educational research.

The Problem

You are the psychologist responsible for program evaluation in a community-based educational facility for severely retarded children. One of the programs attempts to teach these children self-care skills. The literature is not clear whether imitation learning or physically directed learning is the best method for teaching these skills. In imitation learning the child watches the teacher complete a task and then is asked to repeat the task by remembering what the teacher did. In physically directed learning, the teacher actually takes the child and physically guides him through the process. You have directed the staff to place half the children in an imitation learning curriculum for three months and the other half in a physically directed curriculum. Previous research has shown that the learning rates for these children depends upon their intellectual level. Therefore, each subject is matched on intellectual level and one member from each pair is randomly assigned to the imitation learning condition. The other member from the pair is assigned to the physically directed group.

You are interested in detecting whether the physically directed method is better than the imitation method, which makes it a directional test. The data collected are the number of skills learned under each method.

The Solution

The now familiar six-step solution is easily used to solve the problem.

1. Write the null and alternative hypotheses.

Not all textbooks follow the same rules for directional hypotheses. This tutorial adopts a specific way to set up these hypotheses. In this case you expect to find that physically directed learning is better (produces higher scores) than imitation learning. Therefore the alternative hypothesis will indicate that the mean of the second group will be larger than the mean of the first. The null hypothesis must include all other options (i.e., that the mean of the groups are equal and that the mean of group 2 will be smaller than the mean of group 1). Below are these two hypotheses:

$H_o: \mu1 \geq \mu2$
$H_1: \mu1 < \mu2$

2. Set the alpha level.

We'll set the alpha level to .05.

3. Collect the data.

The data for this project are in a file titled *Self Care*, which contains imitation scores and physical guidance scores for twenty-four pairs of children.

4. Calculate the statistic.

The formula for the dependent t is

$$t = \frac{\overline{D}}{S_{\overline{D}}}$$

D is the difference between the scores for each matched pair. In the numerator, $\overline{D}$ is the the average of those differences. In the denominator $S_{\overline{D}}$ is the sample standard deviation of the mean differences.

To obtain the mean difference value ($\overline{D}$), MYSTAT always subtracts the second variable selected in the dialog box from the first. Note that the sign of $\overline{D}$ is affected by the order in which these variables are chosen. It is a good idea to select the variable in the same order as they are written in the alternative hypothesis so that the sign of the mean difference corresponds to the alternative hypothesis. If the sign in the numerator changes, the sign of the *t* value changes.

To calculate the *t* value

1. Select **Ttest** under the **Analyze** menu. The t-test dialog box appears.
2. Make sure that the **Paired** option is selected.
3. Double-click **IMMITATI** in the "Variables" box.

   This is the first variable selected. MYSTAT will subtract the values of the next variable selected from the IMMITATI value to compute the difference scores.

4. Double-click on **PHYSICAL** in the "Variables" box to choose the second variable.

   The physical directed scores will be subtracted from the imitation learning scores.

   The dialog box should look like Figure 6.3.

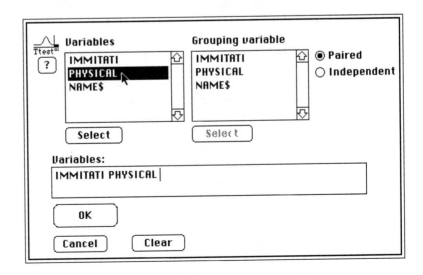

Figure 6.3
Dialog box for a dependent *t*-test

4. Click **OK**.

   You will obtain the results shown in Table 6.3.

Table 6.3
Results from the paired *t*-test

Paired Samples t-test on IMMITATI vs PHYSICAL with 24 cases.
Mean difference = −3.250
SD difference = 3.674
DF = 23
T = −4.333
Prob = 0.000

5. Decide whether or not to reject the null hypothesis.

MYSTAT always reports the probabilities or TYPE 1 errors for two-tailed tests. Thus, for directional tests you must divide the reported probability in half. Then you must check that the mean difference reported occurs in the direction expected by the alternative hypothesis. The *t* value of −4.333 has a low probability of occurring by chance. Remember that 0.000 is output if the probability is less than 0.0005. This value is lower than the alpha set in step 2, so you reject the null hypothesis.

6. Write a summary statement.

The summary statement for this research could be written: "The author found that when teaching self-care skills to severely retarded children a physically-directed method produced significantly better results than an imitation method (t = −4.333, df = 23, p ≤ 0.0005, one-tailed).

One-Sample Situation

In one-sample designs, the dependent *t*-test formula is used when the same people are measured twice. Another name for the one-sample dependent *t*-test is the *paired t-test*. This repeated measures situation occurs when the same subjects are exposed to two different treatments or when pretest and posttest scores are used. The same people are the subjects in both conditions. A one-sample situation requiring a paired *t*-test occurs when the investigator pretests subjects, gives them a treatment designed to change their scores, and then posttests them.

If you are interested in detecting a difference between scores, a nondirectional (two-tailed) approach is appropriate. If you are interested in detecting whether there was an increase (or decrease) in the scores between variables or a difference in the pretest and posttest scores, then a directional (one-tailed) test is needed.

The Problem

You are a biologist interested in the effects of alcohol consumption on maze-running performance in hamsters. You have trained ten hamsters to run a maze until their times show no improvement. After running the maze again as a pretest measure, the rats are given alcohol so that their blood-alcohol levels are proportional to the level that makes humans legally intoxicated. The rats then run the maze a second time, and the results are measured.

You want to detect whether the pretest and posttest times differ. This is a nondirectional (or two-tailed) test. The dependency here is quite evident, the same rats are being measured twice. The paired *t*-test formula is used.

The Solution

The six-step solution follows.

1. Write the null and alternative hypotheses.

Below are these two hypotheses:

$H_o: \mu1 = \mu2$

$H_1: \mu1 \neq \mu2$

The null hypothesis indicates that the pretest scores (time to run the maze before alcohol) are equal to the posttest scores.

2. Set the alpha level.

We'll use .05 again.

3. Collect the data.

The data for this project are so few, it might be valuable to review keyboard entry by typing in this data set. (You will not need to save the file; it is not used elsewhere in this tutorial. If you want to save it, name it *Hamsters*.)

1. Enter the data shown in Figure 6.4.

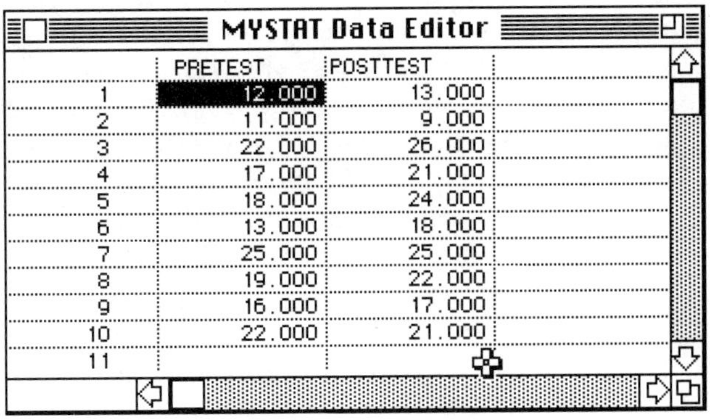

	PRETEST	POSTTEST
1	12.000	13.000
2	11.000	9.000
3	22.000	26.000
4	17.000	21.000
5	18.000	24.000
6	13.000	18.000
7	25.000	25.000
8	19.000	22.000
9	16.000	17.000
10	22.000	21.000
11		

Figure 6.4
The hamster data set

4. Calculate the statistic.

1. Select **Ttest** under the **Analyze** menu.
2. Make sure the **Paired** option is selected.
3. Double-click on **PRETEST** in the "Variables" box.
4. Double-click on **POSTTEST** in the "Variables" box to choose the second variable.

5. Click **OK**.

You should obtain the results shown in Table 6.4.

Table 6.4 Results of the paired *t*-test for the hamster data

Paired Samples t-test on PRETEST vs POSTTEST with 10 cases.

Mean difference	=	-2.100
SD difference	=	2.685
DF	=	9
T	=	-2.473
Prob	=	.035

5. Decide whether or not to reject the null hypothesis.

The *t* value of -2.473 has a lower probability of occurring by chance (.035) than the alpha you set at step 2 (.05). Reject the null hypothesis.

6. Write a summary statement.

The summary statement could be written: "The author found that alcohol consumption in hamsters significantly increased the time it took them to run the maze (*t* = -2.437, df = 9, p = 0.35, two-tailed).

Exercises

1. A large group of learning-disabled college freshmen who experience debilitating anxiety before major tests were matched on an index of test anxiety. Members of these matched pairs were randomly assigned to different groups. The first group was given two weeks of relaxation exercises (RELAX). The second group of students was given two weeks of study skills training (STUDY). Using the data found in the file *Anxiety*, determine whether there is a significant difference between the final exam scores of the two groups. Hand in the printed output if your instructor requests it along with your final summary statement.

2. A vicious debate between behaviorists and traditional medical doctors concerns the merits of using the stimulant Ritalin in treating childhood hyperactivity. A large group of hyperactive children in an urban school system were randomly assigned to either a behavior modification program or a drug therapy program. The data are contained in the file *Hyperactivity*. Determine if there is a significant difference on these children's out-of-seat behavior (OUTSEAT) between the two methods.

3. Divide the *States* data set into two groups (you will need to create a new variable for these groups). The first group is those states east of the Mississippi River. The second group is those states west of the Mississippi. Are there significant differences between their population densities?

4. Using the grouping variable created in exercise 3, are there significant differences between their summer temperatures, winter temperatures, and rainfall amounts? Write summary statements for each.
5. The attitudes toward obtaining an advanced college degree of fifteen undergraduate minority students were measured before and after they participated in a federally funded program designed to increase their awareness of the benefits of a higher degree. The higher the score, the more positive the subject's attitude. The data are contained in the file *Higher Degree*. Did attending the program significantly change their attitudes?
6. Using the *DAC Data* data file, determine whether there has been a change in spending by DAC committee members from 1988 to 1989. Write a summary statement.

7

Analysis of Variance

Two sample *t*-tests determine if there are differences in mean scores between two groups. Analysis of Variance (ANOVA) procedures determine differences among means when there are more than two groups. In ANOVA, grouping variables are referred to as *factors*. If there is a single grouping variable, the procedure is called one-way ANOVA. If there are two grouping variables, the procedure is called two-way ANOVA. With two or more grouping variables, the procedure is called multi-way ANOVA.

Grouping variables or factors are also called the *independent variables* in the research. In true experiments, researchers randomly assign subjects to the different groups. Researchers control the independent variables (they decide who goes into which treatment group). They want to detect whether some measured variable has different values depending upon the group. This measured variable is called the *dependent* variable.

ANOVA is used instead of using multiple *t*-tests to reduce the probability of making a Type 1 error. If you assign subjects to three groups and want to determine if there are differences in the dependent variable between these three groups, using only what you have previously learned, you could conduct a *t*-test comparing group 1 and group 2, then a *t*-test comparing group 1 and group 3, and finally, a third *t*-test comparing group 2 and group 3. However, there is a serious problem with this procedure. If each of the three *t*-tests had alpha levels (Type 1 errors) set at .05, the Type 1 error increases for the experiment when you do three tests in a row. Using ANOVA procedures avoids this Type 1 error inflation.

Objectives

At the end of this tutorial you should be able to
- Determine whether you have a one-way or multi-way ANOVA
- Calculate one-way ANOVA results using MYSTAT
- Calculate two way ANOVA results using MYSTAT

■ One-Way ANOVA Versus Multi-Way ANOVA

Both one-way and multi-way ANOVA procedures are used to decide if three or more sample means are different from one another. To choose between these procedures, determine whether the groups are defined by one or more grouping variables. Figure 7.1 illustrates the decision model for determining if you should choose a one-way or multi-way ANOVA.

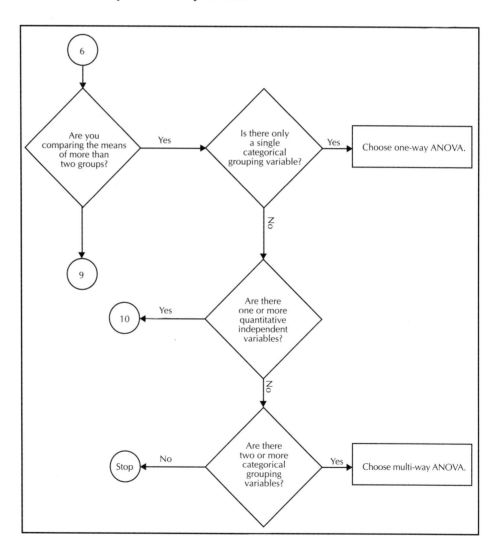

Figure 7.1
Decision model for one-way or multi-way ANOVA

One-Way ANOVA

Figure 7.1 explains that one-way ANOVA is used to detect mean differences among groups when there is a single independent variable and the number of groups formed by that independent (grouping) variable is three or more. One-way ANOVAs are found frequently in the research literature and are one of the most important analysis tools you can learn.

The Problem

You are responsible for determining how different newspaper coupons for your company's product affect sales. You set up four groups. For group 1, a newspaper advertisement without a redemption coupon will be printed. For group 2, the same advertisement will be used with a coupon worth 10 cents. For group 3, the advertisement and a 30-cents coupon will be used. For group 4, the advertisement and a 50-cent coupon will be used. You select twenty communities with daily newspapers within your sales region and randomly assign these communities to your four groups. For each group the local newspaper carries an advertisement for your product in the Wednesday edition. Sales figures from the twenty communities are totaled on the following Saturday (the coupon's expiration date).

The Solution

Below is the six-step solution:

1. Write the null and alternative hypotheses.

In ANOVA, the null and alternative hypotheses are stated somewhat differently. The null hypothesis always assumes that all the groups come from populations with identical means. In this case, the null hypothesis indicates that average sales of your product are the same regardless of the coupon value in the newspaper. The alternative hypothesis is simply that any of the group means differ. Because there are so many possibilities for the alternative hypothesis the null and alternative hypothesis are usually written

$H_0: \mu1 = \mu2 = \mu3 = \mu4$

$H_1:$ not H_0

2. Set the alpha level.

We'll set the alpha level to .05.

3. Collect the data.

The data for this problem are found in the file *Advertisement*.

1. Open the *Advertisement* file on your data disk. When you open the data set, you will notice that there is a variable for the number of products sold (SOLD) and the group to which the community was assigned (GROUP).

4. Calculate the statistic.

1. Select the **ANOVA** command under the **Analyze** menu. The dialog box shown in Figure 7.2 will appear.

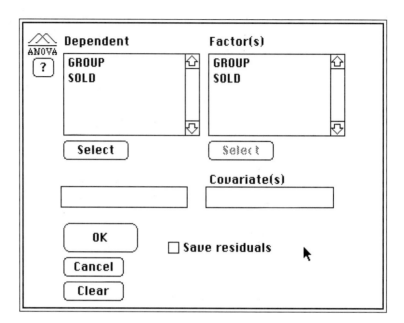

Figure 7.2
ANOVA dialog box

In the "Dependent" box in the upper left of the dialog box, you tell MYSTAT which variable in the data set should be the dependent variable. In this study the dependent variable is the number of products sold (SOLD). In the "Factor(s)" box on the upper right of the dialog box, you select the independent variable or factor. In this example the independent variable GROUP codes the four different treatments. The "Covariate(s)" box is used in Analysis of Covariance (ANCOVA), which is discussed in chapter 10. The **Save residuals** option is for saving *residuals*, which are the deviations of each score from its group mean. For the ANOVA model to be appropriate, these residuals should be normally distributed and have the same variance in every cell.

2. Double-click on **SOLD** in the "Dependent" box.
3. Double-click on **GROUP** in the "Factor(s)" box.

Immediately a second dialog box window (shown in Figure 7.3) appears. In this dialog box you need to indicate the number of groups coded by the grouping variable. There are four groups in this experiment (the four advertisements).

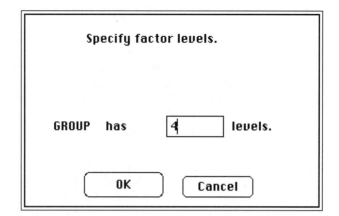

Figure 7.3
Factors dialog box in ANOVA

4. Type the number **4** and click **OK**.

   This dialog box disappears and you are finished with the ANOVA setup. The ANOVA dialog box should look like Figure 7.4.

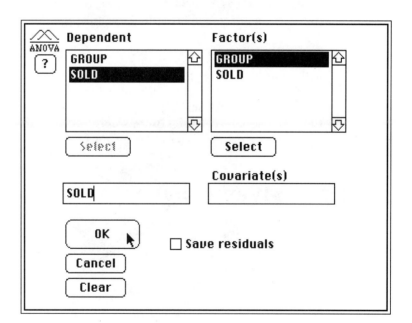

Figure 7.4
The completed ANOVA dialog box

5. Click **OK**.

   The results you should receive are shown in Table 7.1.[1]

Table 7.1
One-way
ANOVA results[2]

Dep var: SOLD   N: 20   Multiple R: .525   Squared multiple R: .275

Analysis of Variance

Source	Sum-of-squares	DF	Mean-square	F-ratio	P
GROUP	15940.000	3	5313.333	2.026	0.151
Error	41960.000	16	2622.500		

In one-way ANOVA two degrees of freedom (DF) are calculated. The first degree of freedom reported is associated with the number of groups in the analysis (number of groups–1). The second is associated with the error term (number of cases–number of groups). In some texts the group degrees of freedom is called the degrees of freedom in the numerator or the degrees of freedom between groups. The degrees of freedom due to error is called the degrees of freedom in the denominator or the degrees of freedom within groups. In every one-way ANOVA, MYSTAT calculates these values for you.

5. Decide whether or not to reject the null hypothesis.

Look at the MYSTAT probability value. Since the p value of 0.151 is larger than the alpha of .05, you fail to reject the null hypothesis.

6. Write a summary statement.

In this case the researcher reports, "Enclosing coupons with the advertisement did not create a significant difference in the sales of the product (F = 2.026, df = 3, 16, p = 0.151)." Remember that the 3 degrees of freedom are used to calculate the mean square between groups and the 16 degrees of freedom are used to calculate the mean square *within* groups.

■ Two-Way ANOVA

Experiments with more than one grouping variable are called factorial designs. Factorial designs are labeled by the number of levels of each factor (grouping variable). For example, assume that you are conducting an experiment to measure the blood pressures of men and women who are either at rest or pedaling stationary bicycles. This is a 2 x 2 (two by two) factorial design. The first factor, SEX, has two levels (Male and Female), and the second factor, EXERCISE, also has two levels (Resting and Pedaling).

There are three things to be measured in this experiment:

1. Does male blood pressure differ from female blood pressure? The test of the SEX main effect answers this question. It is like doing a one-way ANOVA on SEX.
2. Does the blood pressures of people at rest differ from their blood pressures while exercising? The test of the EXERCISE main effect answers this question. It is like doing a one-way ANOVA on EXERCISE.

3. Is the difference between male blood pressure and female blood pressure while resting the same as the difference between their blood pressures while exercising? The test of the interaction between SEX and EXERCISE answers this question. A significant interaction means that differences in resting blood pressures and exercise blood pressures must be described separately for males and females.

The two-way ANOVA procedure addresses all three of these questions.

☞ There isn't any theoretical upper limit to the number of factors or the number of levels in ANOVA designs. However, because the number of tests increases with increases in the independent variables, the results become more difficult to interpret. With every new variable you also need more subjects to create the groups. In business and social sciences, most designs involve two or three factors with four or fewer levels.

The Problem

You are responsible for testing the effectiveness of a drug combined with therapy on schizophrenic patients' behavior. The drug has three dosages (absent, low dosage, high dosage) and the therapy has four types (behavior modification, psychodynamic, group counseling, nondirective). This is referred to as 3 x 4 (read "3 by 4") factorial design because the first factor has three levels and the second factor has four levels. Assume that you have 120 subjects who are randomly assigned to the twelve groups; each group contains ten patients.

The Solution

Work the drug dosage and therapy problem with MYSTAT using the six-step solution.

1. Write the null and alternative hypotheses.

In two-way ANOVA there are three sets of null and alternative hypotheses: one for each factor, and one for the interaction. For main effects there are no differences between the means or there are no treatment effects for that factor. The alternative hypotheses are simply that the null is false. For the interaction hypothesis the null is simply that there is no interaction between the two variables. Again, the alternative is that the null is false. In this tutorial we will state two-way ANOVA hypotheses without symbols.

H_{o1}: The means for the drug dosage groups are all equal.

H_{11}: H_{o1} is false.

H_{o2}: The means for the therapies are all equal.

H_{12}: H_{o2} is false.

H_{o3}: There is no drug dosage by therapy type interaction.

H_{13}: H_{o3} is false.

2. Set the alpha level.

We'll use .05 again for the alpha level.

104 Chapter 7 Analysis of Variance

3. Collect the data.

The data for this problem are found in the file *Schizophrenia*.

1. Open the *Schizophrenia* file on the data disk.

   When you open the data set note that there is a variable for the level of drug, DOSAGE, a variable for the TYPE of therapy, and a variable that indicates the number of behavioral INCIDENTs the person had during the experiment. The fewer behavioral incidents the better the recorded behavior for the individual.

4. Calculate the statistic.

1. Select the **ANOVA** command under the **Analyze** menu. The same dialog box window as in the one-way ANOVA example will appear.

   You want to see the effects on INCIDENT due to DOSAGE and TYPE.

2. Double-click **INCIDENT** as the Dependent variable.
3. Double-click **DOSAGE** as the first Factor.
4. Type 3 for the number of levels in this window, then click **OK**. WARNING: Do **not** click OK in the first dialog box window.
5. Double-click **TYPE** in the "Factor(s)" box.
6. Respond with a **4** when asked for the number of levels for this factor, and click **OK** in this window.

   The ANOVA dialog box should look like Figure 7.5.

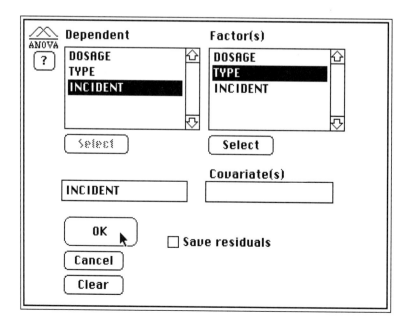

Figure 7.5
Two-way ANOVA dialog box

7. Click **OK**.

The output shown in Table 7.2 should appear.

Table 7.2 Two-way ANOVA results

Dep var: INCIDENT   N: 120   Multiple R: .360   Squared multiple R: .130

Analysis of Variance

Source	Sum-of-squares	DF	Mean-square	F-ratio	P
DOSAGE	2.867	2	1.433	3.448	0.035
TYPE	1.158	3	0.386	0.929	0.430
DOSAGE * TYPE	2.667	6	0.444	1.069	0.386
Error	44.900	108	0.416		

5. **Decide whether or not to reject the null hypothesis.**

In this case you reject the first null hypothesis (Ho_1) and fail to reject the second and third nulls. Again, all you need to do is look at the *p* values and check them against your chosen alpha level.

6. **Write a summary statement.**

For this problem, the researcher might report: "The dosage of the drug administered to the schizophrenics made a difference in the number of behavioral incidents subjects displayed during the experimental period (F = 3.448, df = 2, 108, p = 0.035). No differences due to the type of therapy were detected (F = 0.929, df = 3, 108, p = 0.43). Finally, there was no evidence of an interaction between the dosage level of the drug and the individual's type of therapy (F = 1.069, df = 6, 108, p = 0.386)."

Exercises

1. Use the *States* data set. Divide the states into three regions (you will need to make a variable to code these different regions). The three regions are the East, the Midwest, and the West. Using these groups, are there significant differences in population density, summer temperature, winter temperature, and rainfall. Write summary statements for each of the problems. Your answers may differ from others depending on how you divided the states into the groups.

2. An experimental psychologist is investigating the effect on rats of delta-9 tetrahydrocannabinol (THC) ingestion and their maze-running ability. THC is the psychoactive ingredient in marijuana. The researcher randomly assigns ten rats to four different treatment levels (None = 1, Low = 2, Medium = 3, and High = 4) of THC. After one hour she places each rat into a maze. The time it takes each of the 40 rats to complete the maze (MAZETIME) is

then recorded. The data is found in the file *Rats*. Is there a significant effect on maze-running ability across the THC levels? Write an appropriate summary statement.

3. Travelers from the United States have frequently been warned about eating the foods in foreign countries. The *Herald* magazine in May 1991 reported data from a survey of food available from street venders in Karachi, Pakistan. The survey systematically sampled foods across several different areas in the city. Partial data from that survey are contained in the file *Karachi*. The variables are defined as follows: The type of food (a drink or snack) is labeled FOOD_TY$. The name of the food is labeled FOOD_NA$. The area from which the food was sampled is called AREA. There were eight areas sampled. The bacterial count in the food is called BACTERIA. This variable is measured in colony-forming units per gram of food in powers of 10. Thus if there were 100 colony forming units per gram, a score of 2 (10^2) would be recorded. Finally, the presence of LEAD, ARSENIC, CADMIUM, and CYANIDE are recorded (1 = present, 0 = absent). The report found that only 15.73% of the food sampled in the study was perfectly safe to consume. The safe food was almost exclusively bottled soft drinks. These are referred to in the file as colas. The full report found that 16% of the food was acceptable to eat, 29.21% if eaten would put the person at risk, and 38.95% of the food was dangerous to consume. Use the *Karachi* file and determine if there is a significant difference across the eight areas in bacterial counts. Write a summary statement for your findings.

4. A research psychologist is investigating anorexia nervosa in adolescent females. He wishes to investigate the effects of psychodynamic counseling and behavioristic counseling (COUNSEL) along with three different levels of diet (low calorie = 1, medium calorie = 2, and high calorie = 3) (DIETTYPE) on weight gain (WT_GAIN). Thirty young women with anorexia nervosa are randomly assigned to these six different groups. The weight gain data is found in the file *Anorexia*. Are there main effects for either of the factors? Is there an interaction effect? If requested, answer the questions on the MYSTAT printout and write an appropriate summary statement for a journal article.

5. Using the *Karachi* file, determine whether there is a significant difference between FOOD_TY$ and AREA with respect to bacterial counts. Is there an interaction between the two factors? Write a summary statement for this 2 x 8 ANOVA. You will have to make a new numerical variable for the text variable FOOD_TY$ to use it as a factor.

Notes

[1] There are several terms that have not been defined. In the title line of output, MYSTAT reports the name of the dependent variable and the number of subjects in the experiment. Also given are values for Multiple R and Squared multiple R. These two terms are defined in chapter 9. The Sum-of-squares are used in calculating the ANOVA F statistic. Formulas for sum-of-squares and their interpretations are beyond the scope of this tutorial. If you divide the sum-of-squares by the degrees of freedom (DF) you will obtain the mean squares. Mean squares are variance estimates. The mean square for the factor GROUP estimates the variance in the dependent variable contributed by the treatment plus that contributed by error. The mean square for Error estimates the variance in the dependent variable produced by random error. If you divide the mean square for GROUP by the mean square for Error, you obtain the reported F value.

The mean square for GROUP (often called mean square between groups, MSB) estimates the variance in the dependent variable produced by both treatment effects and error. The mean square for Error (often called the mean square within groups, MSW) estimates the variance in the dependent variable produced by error. The formula for the F statistic is as follows:

$$F = \frac{MSB}{MSW} = \frac{\text{variance due to treatment effects} + \text{random error effects}}{\text{variance due to random error effects}}$$

If the differences in the independent variable (treatment) were not contributing to scatter or variance in the dependent variable, then the two mean squares would both measure the contribution of random error. Therefore, they should be equal, and if you divide them, their value should be 1. If the treatment doesn't produce differences in the dependent variable, then the expected value for the F statistic is 1. F values that are larger than 1 indicate that the independent variable is producing some variation in the dependent variable. If the F value is far enough away from one, you reject the null hypothesis. The p value, as before, alerts you to whether the F statistic is far enough away from its expected value to be considered significant.

[2] The title line of output identifies the dependent variable and the number of subjects in the analysis. Under this title line is the Analysis of Variance source table. The row beginning with the word *Source* lists the origin of the calculated values and the names of the calculations. The row beginning with the word *DOSAGE* reports the statistics associated with the first factor. In this row are the sum-of-squares, degrees of freedom (DF), mean square, F statistic and probability due to the DOSAGE factor. You always compare the p value reported to the alpha level to determine if you reject the null hypothesis. Remember if the p value is less than the alpha level, reject H_0. The next line gives the same information for the second factor (therapy TYPE). The interaction (DOSAGE * TYPE) takes two lines because of the way the interaction effects are abbreviated in the Source column. Finally the error effects are reported. Note that with an alpha of .05, the interaction is nonsignificant, so behavioral incidents are not shown to be jointly produced by dosage and therapy type. The type of therapy is not significant. Dosage is significant.

8

Graphing Data—Two or More Variables

In this chapter you will learn to use the **Plot** command under the **Graph** menu to simultaneously graph two or more variables for each case in a data set. These graphs, called *scatterplots*, visually represent the relationship between two quantitative variables. To produce a scatterplot, the y, or vertical axis, is used to plot the dependent variable, and the x, or horizontal axis, is used to plot the independent variable. The point where these two values intersect for each case in the data set is marked with a dot or another plot symbol. After you have produced several scatterplots, you will be able to make very good guesses about the direction and strength of these relationships.

Objectives

After finishing this tutorial you will be able to

- Produce simple two-variable x–y scatterplots
- Determine whether the data form a functional or statistical relationship
- Detect which individual case produces which scatterplot point and which scatterplot point is associated with which case
- Create scatterplots with fitted regression lines and confidence bands
- Create scatterplots with two variables plotted on the y-axis against a third variable on the x-axis
- Create influence plots
- Create bubble plots
- Set the axis scales
- Overlay several graphs in the view window

■ Two-Variable Scatterplots

Scatterplots are pictures of the relationship between variables. In this tutorial, you will produce a scatterplot showing a simple relationship between two continuous variables. In chapter 2, we created the *School Referrals* file. Assume you are a school psychologist interested in graphically displaying the relationship between the children's scores on the reading test (READ) and their full-scale intelligence quotients (FSIQ). Indeed, in psychology, intelligence quotients (IQs) are primarily used to predict academic achievement scores.

After you have opened the *School Referrals* file, the following steps will produce the scatterplot:

1. Select the **Plot** command under the **Graph** menu.
2. Double-click on **READ** (the dependent variable) in the "Y Variables" box. (You will need to scroll down the list.)

    There are no mandates for determining which of the two variables is called the dependent variable and which is called the independent variable. However, if you are going to use one variable to predict values for the other, the variable used to predict is referred to as the *predictor* variable and it becomes the independent variable in the study. The variable with estimated values is called the *criterion* variable and it becomes the dependent variable in the study. The achievement variable (**READ**) is the logical choice for the criterion variable because this is what FSIQ predicts. Traditionally, criterion variables are graphed along the *y*-axis.

3. Double-click on **FSIQ** (the independent variable) in the "X Variables" box. Leave all the other defaults options alone. Your dialog box should look like Figure 8.1.

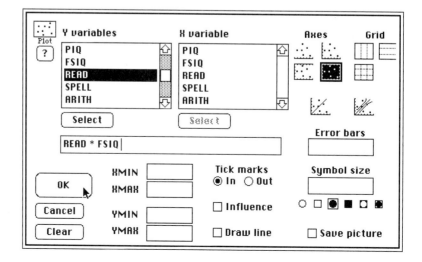

Figure 8.1
Plot dialog box

4. Click **OK**.

Your output should look like Figure 8.2.

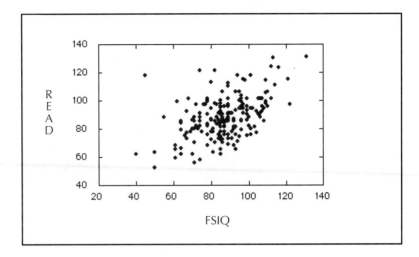

Figure 8.2
Scatterplot of FSIQ predicting READ

You have created a scatterplot for two variables.

☞ You can print graphs after they have been constructed. Just make sure the View window is active (click on the View window if you are not sure) and chose **Print graph...** from the **File** menu.

Scatterplot Interpretation

Relationships between continuous variables differ in direction and strength. These relationships can be visualized using scatterplots. If it is a *linear relationship,* that is if a straight line can approximate this relationship, then the *Pearson product-moment correlation coefficient,* or simply the *correlation,* is a number that describes the relationship. You can determine the direction of the correlation by looking at the general orientation of the scatterplot. If smaller values for the *x* variable are frequently paired with smaller values for the *y* variable and larger values for the *x* variable are paired with larger values for the *y* variable, the scatterplot will run from the lower-left corner of the graph to the upper-right corner. This indicates a positive relationship—as one variable's values become larger, the other variable's values also become larger. If smaller values for the *x* variable are frequently paired with larger values and larger *x* values are paired with smaller *y* values, the scatterplot will run from the upper-left corner to the lower-right corner of the graph. This indicates a negative relationship. In chapter 9 we will use MYSTAT to calculate the Pearson correlation coefficient between variables. If the relationship is positive, the correlation will be a positive number; if the relationship is negative, the correlation will be negative. Figures 8.3a–b illustrate the directions of scatterplots.

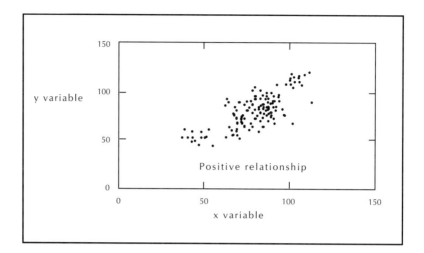

Figure 8.3a
Scatterplot with a positive relationship

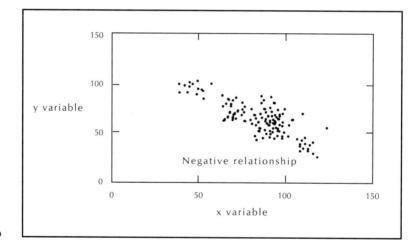

Figure 8.3b
Scatterplot with a negative relationship

What is the direction of the relationship in Figure 8.2 between FSIQ and READ?

The second component of a relationship is its strength, which indicates the closeness of the relationship. Scatterplots are excellent tools for estimating the strength of a relationship. Pearson product-moment correlations measure the strength of linear relationships. If all the data points fit exactly on a straight line, then the relationship is perfect, and the correlation equals ±1 (depending on the direction). If the data points do not create a linear pattern, there is not a linear relationship and the Pearson correlation equals zero. Figures 8.4a–d depict different linear relationships.

What would you guess the correlation to be for Figure 8.2? Would it be closer to .70 or closer to 0.0?

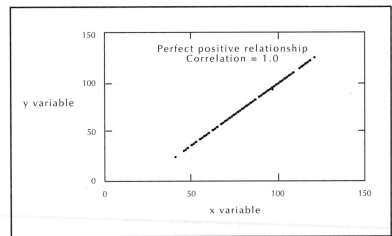

Figure 8.4a
Scatterplot of a perfect positive relationship

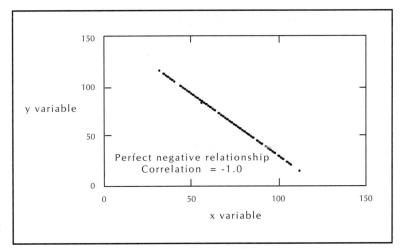

Figure 8.4b
Scatterplot of a perfect negative relationship

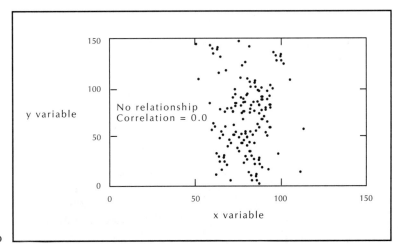

Figure 8.4c
Scatterplot in which there is no relationship

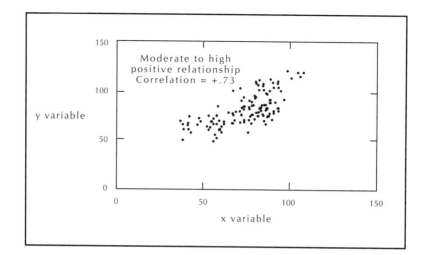

Figure 8.4d
Scatterplot of a moderate positive relationship

One advantage of using scatterplots is that you can sometimes see relationships that the Pearson correlation underestimates. Pearson correlations underestimate relationships that aren't linear. Figure 8.5 illustrates data that can be perfectly matched by a sine curve pattern. The Pearson correlation for this data is given in Figure 8.5. Your eyes can detect the strong relationship; the Pearson correlation cannot.

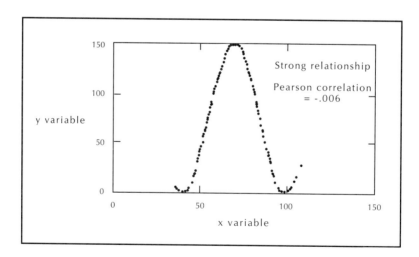

Figure 8.5
Scatterplot of a sine curve pattern

■ Functional and Statistical Relationships

When every value of one variable (x) determines a unique value of another (y), the two variables are said to have a functional relationship. For example, if y is the dependent variable and x is the independent variable, and y is determined by $y = 2x$, then a functional relationship exists. When graphs show functional relationships, the points all fall directly on the function line or curve. Figure 8.6 is a graph of the functional relationship $y = \sqrt{x}$.

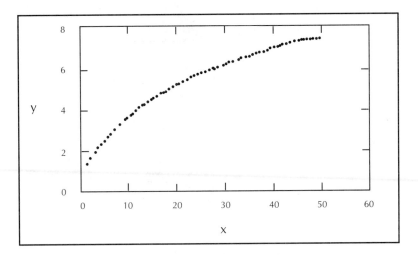

Figure 8.6
Scatterplot of $y = \sqrt{x}$

Statistical relationships are not perfect. When you look at the graph of a statistical relationship, the data points will not fall perfectly on a line or curve (see Figures 8.2, 8.3a, 8.3b, 8.4c, 8.4d).

■ Identifying Scatterplot Data Points

Another advantage of producing scatterplots is that data points far away from the majority are easily detected. These outside values are called *outliers*. Outliers are isolates in the data swarm. In the scatterplot you produced in Figure 8.2, the point by itself in the upper left-hand quadrant of the graph is an outlier.

Outliers are often caused by errors in data entry. For example, the researcher might type **1400** instead of the correct value of **140**. If outliers are not produced by a data entry error, they are often unique cases in the data set and are worthy of individual study to determine why they are so different.

It is important to discover which case in the data set produced which point in the scatterplot and vice versa. With scatterplots, MYSTAT provides two cursors in the View window that allow you to detect these cases. Look at the top two symbols in the upper-left corner of your View window. These symbols are called the *Scatterplot brushing tools*. The top symbol (left pointing arrow) allows you to click on a data point in the View window and identify the case that produced this point in the Data Editor. The next symbol (the flashlight) allows you to find data points in the View window after they have been selected in the Data Editor. The bottom symbol is the standard MYSTAT cursor you have used throughout this tutorial. When the View window is active you can select between the three cursors by clicking once on the appropriate symbol. The scatterplot brushing tools are shown in Figure 8.7.

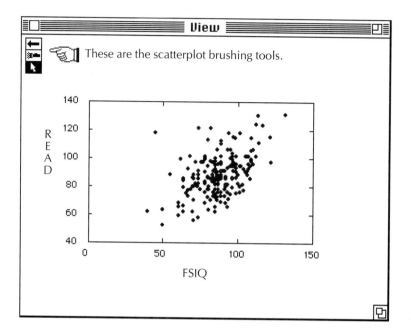

Figure 8.7
The scatterplot brushing tools

Scatterplot Brushing: Left Arrow

The left arrow brushing tool is used to find which case is associated with which data point.

To identify a data point, do the following:

1. With the scatterplot of FSIQ predicting READ showing in the View window (see Figure 8.2), click on the left arrow in the View window.

   The cursor should change to the left arrow symbol when you move the mouse.

2. While the tip of the arrow head is directly on the outlier in the upper left quadrant, click and hold the mouse button down.

   Your view window should look like Figure 8.8 while you are holding the mouse button down.

3. Click on the Data Editor window to activate it.

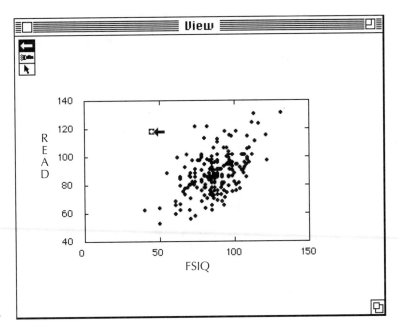

Figure 8.8
Clicking on the outlier

One of the cells in case 182 is highlighted (it doesn't matter which cell). This is the case that produced the outlier. In this data set, case 182 is a child diagnosed as having Laurence-Moon-Biedl syndrome. This degenerative disease is probably caused by recessive mutations of two genes in the same chromosome. It is far more frequent in males. It is characterized by girdle-type obesity, hypogenitalism, mental retardation, polydactyly, skull deformations, pigmentary retinal degeneration, and generally a shortened life-span. This child was in third grade at the time his data were collected. He could do some academic tasks but had no comprehension of what he was doing. His FSIQ places him in the trainable mentally retarded range, but his READ score is above average. This highly unlikely event is explained by the fact that the reading test only asked children to pronounce words. This youngster could read individual words, but hadn't a clue as to their meanings. The numbers that produce the outlier are correct, and the case is interesting because of the child's unique qualities.

Scatterplot Brushing: Flashlight

What if you want to find out which case produced which point in the plot? The flashlight tool performs this task. Look at the data set and notice that cases 65, 66, and 67 all belong to group 3 (the nonhandicapped group). Because they are all in the nonhandicapped group, you would expect them to be near the area where values of 100 (average values in the population) occur on both axes.

To find these cases in the scatterplot, do the following:

1. Click in the Data Editor window to make it the active window.

2. Highlight cases 65, 66, and 67 in the data set by pointing to them with the regular cursor and then dragging through them.
3. Activate the View window by clicking in it.
4. Choose the flashlight tool by clicking on it.
5. Point anywhere inside the View window and press and hold down the mouse button.

These three cases are highlighted in the scatterplot as shown in Figure 8.9. Note that on your screen, the cases are simply highlighted by a box. So that you can easily locate them in the figure, the flashlight is pointing directly at them and a circle has been drawn around them. The data points make up an approximate right triangle in the lower middle of the scatterplot. The positions are where one would expect non-handicapped children to perform on an intelligence test (see Figure 8.9).

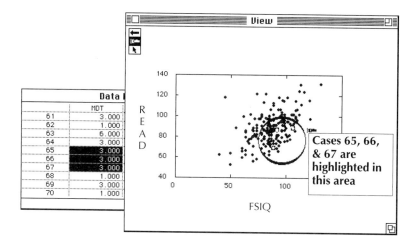

Figure 8.9
Using the flashlight

The Flashlight and Multiple Data Points

You can rapidly find interesting cases by combining the **Find case...**, **Find next**, and **Complex find...** commands with the flashlight. (**Find case...** and **Find next...** are under the Editor menu; **Complex Find...** is in the **Find case...** dialog box.) The **Find case...** command allows you to find cases that meet certain specifications. After you find the first case that meets the specifications, the **Find next** command will find the next case meeting the same specifications.

To find all the children who scored over eleven points on the AGGRESS variable in the scatterplot:

1. Click in the Data Editor window to make it active, then scroll to the top.

Identifying Scatterplot Data Points **119**

This makes sure you are starting from the top of the data file and will find all the relevant cases.

2. Click in the View window with the scatterplot to make it active.
3. Click on the flashlight tool.
4. Select **Find case...** from the **Editor** menu.
5. Complete the dialog box so that you find the cases in which AGGRESS is greater than eleven. The completed dialog box is shown in Figure 8.10.

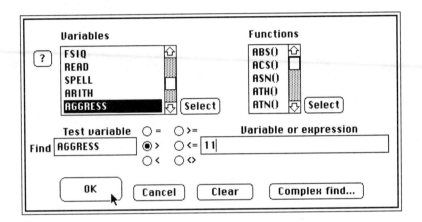

Figure 8.10
Completed **Find case...** dialog box

6. Click **OK**.
7. Click and hold the mouse down anywhere in the View window using the flashlight cursor. You will see a highlighted case in the scatterplot at approximately 60 on the *x*-axis and 70 on the *y*-axis. The area in which it is located is shown within the circle next to the flashlight in Figure 8.11. This is the data point associated with the first case where AGGRESS is greater than eleven.
8. Select **Find next** from the **Editor** menu.
9. Click the flashlight to see the next case.

The second youngster whose AGGRESS score is above eleven is in the upper-right portion of the graph. Instead of selecting the **Find next** command using the mouse and the Editor menu, you may also press the command key [⌘] and the [N] key at the same time. Repeat steps 7 and 8 until the message in Figure 8.12 appears, then click **OK**. There should be 17 children who score over 11 points on AGGRESS.

120   Chapter 8   *Graphing Data — Two or More Variables*

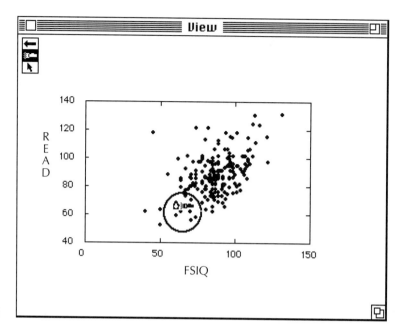

Figure 8.11
The first data point in which AGGRESS > 11

Figure 8.12
Dialog box stating that no more cases can be found that meet the specifications in the **Find case...** command

Complex find... allows you to join different search strategies with either a logical **And** or **Or**. If the strategies are joined with an **And**, both expressions must be true for the case to be found. If the search strategies are joined with an **Or**, either strategy can be true and the case will be found.

To find a youngster in the scatterplot whose FSIQ is greater than 130 and who is also aggressive:

1. Make the Data Editor active and scroll to the top of the Data Editor window.

2. Make the View window active and choose the flashlight tool.
3. Select **Find case...** from the **Editor** menu.
4. Click once in the **Complex find...** button in the lower-right portion of the dialog box.

   A second dialog box will appear. You need to type the search strategies and connect them with either an **And** or **Or**.
5. Type **AGGRESS > 11** in the **"Find"** box.
6. Click the **And** box.

   The first search strategy equation will be moved to the large box on the lower-right side of the dialog box; the **And** connector will be appended to the end.
7. Type **FSIQ > 130** into the "Find" box.

   Your completed **Complex find...** dialog box should look like Figure 8.13.

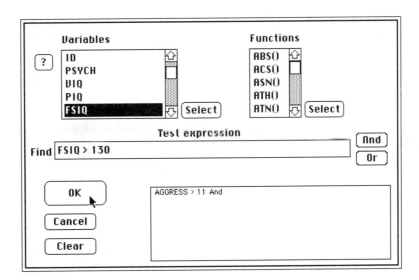

Figure 8.13
The completed **Complex find...** dialog box

8. Click **OK**.

   When you click the flashlight tool in the View window, the cases that meet the criterion will be highlighted. In this case, there is only one youngster in the data set who is considered gifted and overly aggressive (see Figure 8.14). There were only twelve children who received higher scores than this youngster on the AGGRESS variable. You might remember that the mean AGRESS score is about 4 points and the most points any youngster received on this scale was 20.

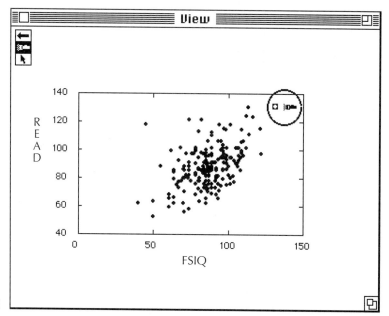

Figure 8.14
A gifted aggressive child

WARNING: *You should now select the regular cursor tool. If you leave the flashlight selected, you may get a message later that you are out of memory for scatterplot brushing. If such a message appears, click **OK** and everything will proceed normally.*

■ Producing Scatterplots with Regression Lines

A *regression line* is the best straight line for predicting the *y* values from the *x* values in a scatterplot. If you draw your own line through the data swarm, then compute the vertical distance between the line and the dot for every case, square that distance, and then add the squared values together, you will get a number (sum of squared residuals) that indicates how closely your line fits the data. For all possible lines through the swarm, the best predicting line has the smallest sum of squared residuals. Figure 8.15 illustrates two cases to be squared and summed to get the value for the line. No other straight line would fit better (give a smaller value for these squares) than the regression line. The *Pearson product-moment correlation* measures how closely the data values match this straight regression line.

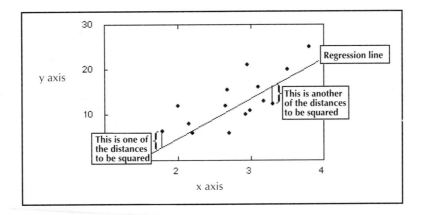

Figure 8.15
Scatterplot with the regression line

To get a feel for how regression lines for other samples from the same population might fall, you can find the confidence interval for the regression line using the sample being graphed. *Confidence intervals* are formed by hyperbolic bands (curved like a hyperbola) around the actual regression line. If the residuals are normally distributed and have equal variance at all locations along the *x*-axis, and if you chose a 95% confidence interval, then you could say that 95 times out of 100, the computed bands would surround the regression line in the population from which these data were sampled.

For a simple regression line, click on the icon in the upper-right corner of the **Plot** dialog box with the single regression line drawn through the data swarm. To draw confidence intervals around the regression line click that option. If you choose the confidence interval option, MYSTAT will ask you to specify a percentage value for the confidence interval. The usual percentage values chosen by researchers are 68, 95, or 99. Figure 8.16 shows where these options are located on the **Plot** dialog box.

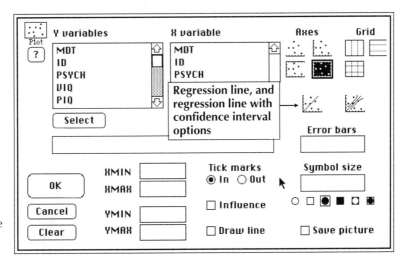

Figure 8.16
Plot dialog box showing the regression line option and the regression line with confidence interval option

To produce a regression line with 95% confidence intervals for FSIQ predicting ARITH in the *School Referrals* data set:

1. Select **Plot** from the **Graph** menu.
2. Double-click on **ARITH** in the "Y variables" box.
3. Double-click on **FSIQ** in the "X variable" box.
4. Click once on the symbol for a regression line with confidence intervals (see Figure 8.16).

   A second dialog box should appear. Here you tell MYSTAT the confidence interval you want around the regression line.
5. Type the number **95** into this second dialog box. It should look like Figure 8.17.

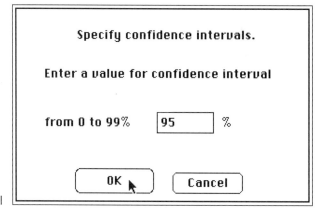

Figure 8.17
The second dialog box used to enter the percentage value for the confidence interval

You are indicating that you want to place 95% confidence intervals around the regression line.

6. Click **OK**.

   This dialog box should look like Figure 8.18. The regression with confidence intervals symbol is dark, indicating that you chose this option.
7. Click **OK**.

   ☞ When you see the Overlay alert, choose **Next plot**.

   The plot in Figure 8.19 should appear.

There are several differences between this scatterplot and the one in Figure 8.2. In Figure 8.19 (1) the criterion variable (graphed on the y-axis) was changed from READ to ARITH, (2) there is a single straight regression line drawn through the data swarm, (3) there are two curved (hyperbolic) confidence intervals drawn around the regression line, and (4) the regression equation is produced at the bottom of the graph.

Producing Scatterplots with Regression Lines

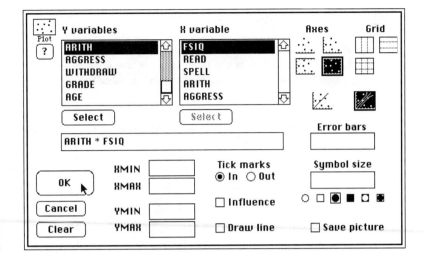

Figure 8.18
The **Plot** dialog box using ARITH and FSIQ and a regression line with confidence intervals

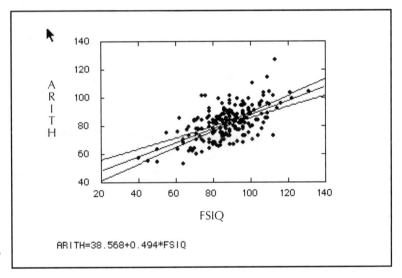

Figure 8.19
Plot output with regression line and 95% confidence intervals

You may remember from math class that any straight line can be formed by the general equation $y = mx + b$ where m stands for the *slope* of the line and b is the *constant* or *intercept*. Regression lines are no exception, and MYSTAT gives you the equation for the regression line in the form $y = b + mx$. At the bottom of Figure 8.19, you see that ARITH is the y variable, b = 38.568 and m = 0.494, and the x or predictor variable is FSIQ. To determine any point on the regression line, start with 38.568 and add to that value 0.494 times the FSIQ value. For example, if FSIQ = 100, then the regression line passes through (38.568 + .494*100) 87.968 on the y-axis. Look at Figure 8.19 and note that the regression line does appear to pass through these two points.

■ Influence Plots

As noted earlier, outliers in correlation studies are often problematic. To visualize the influence a case has on the scatterplot, you need to produce an *influence plot*. An influence plot scales the size of each point in the scatterplot according to its influence on the correlation coefficient.

To produce an influence plot you must select the **influence** option in the plot dialog box. See the lower middle column of the dialog box in Figure 8.18.

To produce an influence plot of **READ** on the *y*-axis and **FSIQ** on the *x*-axis using the *School Referrals* data, do the following:

1. Select **Plot** from the **Graph** menu.
2. Double-click on **READ** in the "Y variables" box.
3. Double-click on **FSIQ** in the "X variable" box.
4. Click once in the small square to the left of the **Influence** option.
5. Click **OK**.

Your plot should look like Figure 8.20.

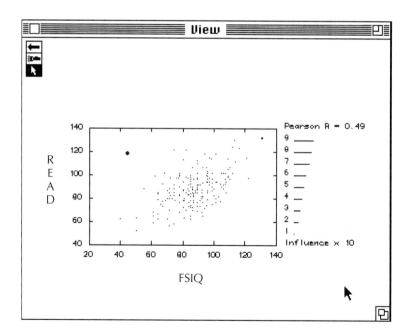

Figure 8.20
Influence plot using READ and FSIQ

The outlier is much larger than the other points in the plot, indicating that it has undue influence on the correlation. When outliers have undue influence on the correlation coefficient, they adversely influence the regression equation. The data point with the undue influence is case 182, the Laurence-Moon-Biedl youngster. If you forget which case produces this influential dot, the scatterplot brushing tools can be used.

In the upper-right corner of the output, notice that the Pearson product-moment correlation is calculated. In this example the value is 0.49. Just outside the right margin of the graph is a scale for determining the influence of each point. It appears that case 182 is about 20 times more influential than any other case. The width of this dot is approximately the same length as the line next to the 2 in the influence scale.

■ Bubble Plots

Another method for displaying three variables on a two-dimensional grid is to produce a *bubble plot*. Bubble plots allow you to scale the size of the scatterplot dots according to some appropriately scaled numeric variable. This third variable changes in relation to the other two variables that determine the position of the dot. To have the third variable determine the size of the scatterplot points, you type the variable's name in the **Symbol size** box in the **Plot** dialog box window. The variable used in the "Symbol size" box must have values of an appropriate size or the plot will be meaningless.

Using the *School Referrals* data, you will produce a bubble plot of VIQ on the *y*-axis and PIQ on the *x*-axis with WITHDRAW determining the size of the symbols.

WARNING: *If you try this without any changes, your plot will be meaningless. The numeric variable that goes in the "Symbol size" box indicates how much larger or smaller the symbol is compared to the default. If you used WITHDRAW without any adjustment, some of your symbols could be almost 50 times larger than the default size. Points this big would blot out the entire scatterplot. You must therefore rescale WITHDRAW.*

To complete the bubble plot, load the *School Referrals* data and follow these steps:

1. Scroll to the top of the Data Editor window.
2. To rescale WITHDRAW, create a new variable by typing **NW** into the first empty space in the variable-naming row.
3. To enter values for NW, use the **Math** command and set **NW** to **WITHDRAW/20**.

    With this new variable the symbol size for someone with a WITHDRAW of 40 will be twice the default size.

4. Select **Plot** from the **Graph** menu.
5. Double-click **VIQ** in the "Y variables" box.
6. Double-click **PIQ** in the "X variable" box.
7. Type the name of the new variable (**NW**) into the "Symbol size" box.

    ☞ You cannot double-click for this step; you must type the variable's name into the "Symbol size" box.

8. Click **OK**.

Your output should look like Figure 8.21.

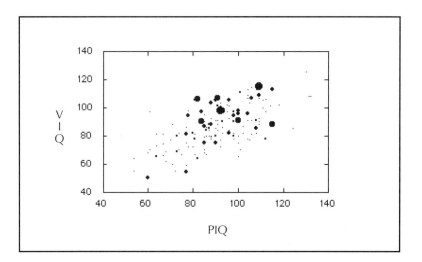

Figure 8.21
Output from a bubble plot

Notice that VIQ and PIQ are highly correlated. Moreover, withdrawn students tend to have higher verbal and somewhat higher performance scores.

■ Other Plot Dialog Box Options

Like the other graph commands that send output to the View window, the Plot dialog box allows you to set minimum and maximum values for the axis scales. We discussed the MIN and MAX options briefly in chapter 3. Because the Plot command uses two variables, minimums and maximums can be set separately for each with the options **XMIN**, **XMAX**, **YMIN**, or **YMAX**. MYSTAT does a good job in selecting the scales along the axes so that the View window is filled with points. You may want to set your own limits when you want to force scales to begin at zero, when you want to make the range of the scales the same for two or more plots, and when you want to zoom in on a small region of the plot. You can also select the number of axes and type of grid you want displayed. To eliminate any unwanted axes or grids, click off the highlighted options.

Other **Plot** options that haven't been discussed include the "Error bars" box, the plot "Symbols size" choices and the **Draw line** option. If you type a variable name in the "Error bars" box, MYSTAT will use the value for that variable to produce error bars around each data point. This option is discussed in chapter 9. The plot "Symbols size" choices in the lower-right part of the dialog box allow you to change the shape of the plotting symbol. Click on the shape you want. Finally, the **Draw line** option draws a line connecting the points in the scatterplot. This option is useful for producing line graphs.

■ Overlaying Graphs

When you produce two graphs in sequence without closing the View window, you see the Overlay alert (see Figure 3.6). So far, you have always chosen **Next plot** when you see that alert. To overlay two graphs, or to put two or more graphs in the View window so they may be seen simultaneously, choose the **Overlay plot** option in overlay alert. When the **Overlay plot** option is used, the View window is not erased before the next graph is plotted. If you resize and move the graphs, they will not overlap and you can clearly see them all. This option is useful when you want to use two different graph types together. Frequently, a one-variable plot (i.e., a box plot or histogram) will be overlaid on a scatterplot. The box plot or histogram is used to visualize the distribution of the single variable graphed on either the x- or y-axis.

With the *School Referrals* data, you will produce a scatterplot of FSIQ predicting READ scores. Then you will illustrate the distribution of each of these single variables with a box plot placed along the correct axis orientation.

1. Select **Plot** from the **Graph** menu.
2. Double-click on **READ** in the "Y variables" box and **FSIQ** in the "X variable" box, then click **OK**.

   This creates the same plot you produced at the beginning of this tutorial (see Figure 8.2). Next you want to show a box plot of FSIQ along the x-axis. This box plot will depict the distribution of FSIQ along the axis used to plot this variable.

3. Place the cursor arrow directly above the upper-left corner of the plot frame at the top of the y-axis and drag the cursor up and to the right until the right side of the flickering box aligns with the right side of the scatterplot. When you let go of the mouse button, the flickering box disappears. Figure 8.22 shows the View window with the resized area. (For further details see "Resizing Graphs" in chapter 3.)

   The height of this box is not as critical as the length and position of the box. You want the next plot to be scaled the same as the x-axis in the scatterplot.

   ☞ If the cursor looks like a hand, you have moved the cursor inside the plot frame. Move the cursor outside the plot frame until the cursor looks like an arrow.

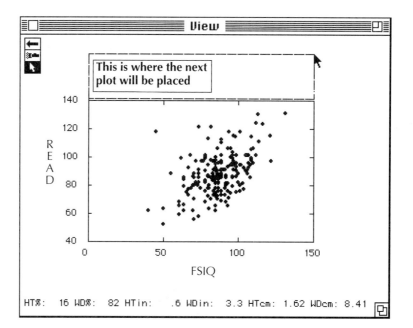

Figure 8.22
Dragging the Resize area for the next plot

4. Select **Box** from the **Graph** menu. Double-click on **FSIQ,** the variable plotted on the *x*-axis, in the "Variables" box. Click off all **Axes** options.

You need to turn off the axes options for the box plot so they don't interfere with the axes already drawn in the scatterplot. The resizing for your box plot is exactly as long as the scatterplot was wide, so its scale is appropriate for your box plot. Figure 8.23 shows the completed dialog box for this step.

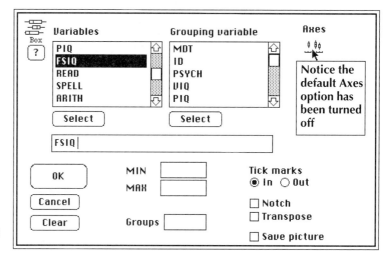

Figure 8.23
Completed dialog box for the box plot

5. Click **OK**.
6. Select **Overlay plot** in the Overlay alert. See Figure 8.24.

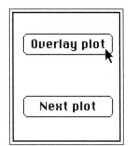

Figure 8.24
Click on Overlay plot

The View window will not be erased and the box plot will be drawn in the area you indicated. Your output should look like Figure 8.25.

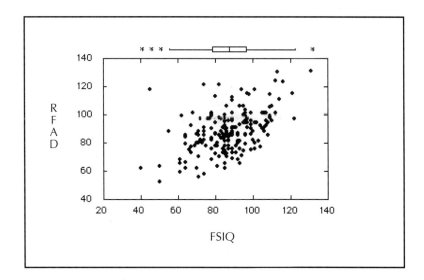

Figure 8.25
The scatterplot and box plot together

This overlaid scatterplot contains more information than the scatterplot itself. You can not only see where the median and the first and third quartile scores fall but also where the points for very low and high values fall.

If you want to do any more plots, you should reset the size of the plotting window. Use the same method as before. Put the cursor about an inch above and to the right of the lower-left corner of the View window and drag the flickering box to the size of the next plot you want to draw. Then release the mouse button.

Exercises

1. Produce a scatterplot from the School Referrals file that uses VIQ to predict SPELL scores. Look at the two extreme outliers in the scatterplot on the SPELL variable. What two cases produced these scores? (Use the left arrow.)

2. Along the top of the scatterplot overlay a box-and-whiskers plot of VIQ. In the right margin, overlay a box-and-whiskers plot of SPELL. (To get the graph size back to the default, you can quit MYSTAT or remember to re-size the graph so that your next scatterplot will be drawn in the correct area.) To change the orientation of the box plot for SPELL, you will need to use the **Transpose** option in the **Box** dialog box. Your overlaid scatterplot should look like Figure 8.26.

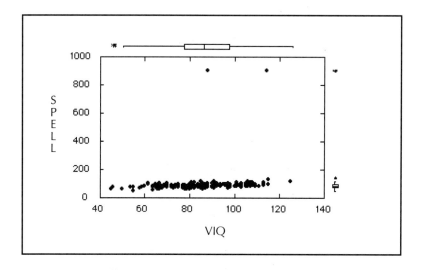

Figure 8.26
Overlaid scatterplot

3. If the SPELL scores must range from 45 to 145, what is the likely cause of these outliers?

4. Correct these scores to read 90 on SPELL, save the corrected data set as *School Referrals Corr*, and produce a corrected scatterplot of VIQ predicting SPELL.

5. Produce a scatterplot of VIQ predicting ARITH with AGGRESS determining the size of the scatterplot symbol. Does the scatterplot indicate that AGGRESS is related to VIQ and ARITH?

WARNING: *You will need to create a new variable for AGGRESS, since it ranges from 0 to 20 in the original data file. A scatterplot symbol twenty times as large as the default will blot out most of the scatterplot. Experiment with different values. A variable in which AGGRESS is divided by five works nicely.*

6. Delete all the cases from the *School Referrals* data set that have FSIQ > 110 and FSIQ < 85. Save this data set as *School Referrals Deleted*. Construct a scatterplot in which FSIQ is on the *x*-axis and READ is on the *y*-axis. Does

the shape of the scatterplot change from the first time these variables were graphed? Why or why not? (Hint: Use the **Recode** command.)

7. Using the *States* file, produce a scatterplot between population density and summer temperature. Is there a linear relationship between these two variables?

8. When ocean navigators use sextants and the sun to find their position, they must correct their sextant readings using a Dip correction. These Dip values change depending on the height of the observer's eye above the water. Thus, a navigator on a small ship close to the water's surface would use a different correction value than a person standing on the deck of a large freighter. A table of Dip corrections is provided in the file *Dips*. Plot the correction (DIP) on the *y*-axis against the height of eye (HEIGHT) on the *x*-axis. Is there a relationship between these values? Is this relationship best described by a line or a curve? Is this a functional or statistical relationship?

9. Rank the *Dips* data using only the DIP variable in the ranking. Title this new file *Dips Ranked*. Plot the ranked DIP on the *y*-axis against HEIGHT on the *x*-axis. Is the relationship changed by the rank ordering of this single variable? If so, describe the change.

10. Rank the *Dips Ranked* data using HEIGHT as the ranking variable. Title this new file *Dips Ranked Ranked*. Now both DIP and HEIGHT are in rank order. Plot DIP on the *y*-axis and HEIGHT on the *x*-axis. Has the relationship changed when both variables are in rank order? If so, describe the change.

9

Correlation and Regression

In this chapter you will learn to use the **Corr** and **Regress** commands under the **Analyze** menu. As noted in chapter 8, a correlation coefficient measures the strength of association between variables. A value of zero indicates that there is no association. Values of either −1 or +1 indicate perfect associations between the variables. The **Regress** command computes *bivariate* (one predictor and one criterion) and *multiple regression* (more than one predictor and one criterion) solutions. While you were able to produce Pearson product-moment correlations and regression equations using the **Plot** command in chapter 8, the **Corr** command computes correlations between many pairs of variables and other correlations like the Spearman rank correlation. The **Regress** command computes estimates of regression coefficients and tests their significance.

Objectives

At the end of this chapter you should be able to

- Determine whether to calculate a Pearson correlation or a Spearman correlation
- Determine whether to conduct a regression analysis
- Calculate Pearson correlations between any two numeric variables
- Calculate Spearman correlations and understand the difference between the Pearson and Spearman correlations
- Compute and interpret bivariate regression analyses
- Compute and interpret multiple regression analyses
- Detect outliers in regression analysis and understand Cook's D statistic, leverage estimates, and studentized residuals

Determining Whether to Use Corr or Regress

Correlations are for measuring association, regression is for prediction. As we said in chapter 8, the Pearson product-moment correlation coefficient is a number that measures the linear relationship between quantitative variables. The **Corr** command computes Pearson correlations and other correlations that use the same formula. The other correlations have various names, but because they all use the same formula they are considered to be in the "Pearson family."

The *Spearman rank correlation* is a number that measures the relationship between rank-ordered variables. It is simply a Pearson correlation on data whose quantitative values are replaced by their rank orders.

The other Pearson family coefficients all involve one or more dichotomous variables. *Dichotomous variables*, also called binary variables, have only two values. The **Corr** command produces correlations between dichotomous variables, but it does not test them for statistical significance. Therefore, the **Corr** results will generally be used for descriptive purposes.

The **Regress** command enables you to use the value of the predictor variable to estimate the criterion value. If you use a single predictor to estimate a single criterion, you are conducting a *bivariate regression*. If you use several predictors to estimate a single criterion, you are executing a *multiple regression*. **Regress** conducts the necessary inferential statistics and provides the regression equation. Figure 9.1 illustrates the decision model for determining whether to use the **Corr** command to calculate a Pearson or Spearman correlation or the **Regress** command to conduct bivariate or multiple regressions.

Correlation Coefficients

There are many correlation coefficients available to researchers. The two most popular are the Pearson product-moment correlation coefficient (named after the statistician Karl Pearson) and the Spearman rank coefficient (named after the British psychologist Charles Spearman). Traditionally, the Pearson correlation has been used to indicate the degree of association between two continuous variables, while the Spearman correlation has been used to indicate the degree of association between two variables that are ranks. As you will discover, these two correlations may actually use the same formula. There are several other correlations that also employ the Pearson formula. Two that you should know are the *point biserial* correlation (r_{pb}) in which one of the variables is measured as a dichotomy and the other is continuous, and the *phi* (ϕ) coefficient in which both variables are measured as dichotomies.

Correlation Coefficients **137**

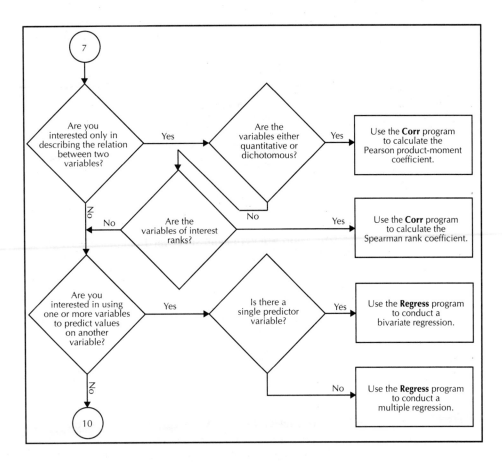

Figure 9.1
Decision model for
Corr and **Regress**

Pearson Product-Moment Correlation

The Pearson product-moment correlation is symbolized in most textbooks with an *r* and is appropriate when both variables are continuous. If one or more variables are dichotomous, the same steps and the same formula are used to calculate the correlation. The only difference is that the name of the coefficient changes.

Calculation of *r*

To measure the degree to which several variables in the *School Referrals* file are related, you will calculate the Pearson correlations between each of them.

To produce this Pearson correlation matrix:

1. Open the *School Referrals* data set.
2. Choose the **Corr** command under the **Analyze** menu.
3. When the dialog box window is shown, select **VIQ**, **PIQ**, **FSIQ**, **READ**, **SPELL**, **ARITH**, **AGGRESS**, and **WITHDRAW** by

sequentially double-clicking on them in the "Variables" box. Your dialog box should look like Figure 9.2.

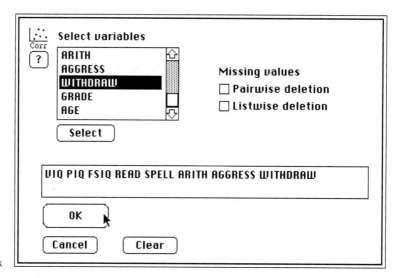

Figure 9.2
Correlation dialog box

These are the variables that will be used by the **Corr** program for calculating the coefficients. If you do not choose any variables, MYSTAT calculates correlations between every numeric variable. **Corr** calculates a correlation for each possible pair of variables selected. The correlation for any variable with itself is always +1.0. If all the possible correlations were calculated regardless of the order of the variables, these values could be placed in a square table or matrix. Figure 9.3 illustrates this square matrix. Note that a 1.0 is placed in each cell in which a variable is correlated with itself (on the diagonal).

The correlation between any pair of variables is the same no matter what the order. For example, the correlation between VIQ and PIQ (.65) is identical to that between PIQ and VIQ. Because the correlation does not change when the order of the variables changes, this square matrix can be divided into two triangular matrices. The upper-right triangle of this matrix (shaded) provides the same information as the lower-left triangular matrix. Each column in the lower-left triangle contains values identical to those of the corresponding row in the upper-right triangle. Therefore, both triangles are not required. MYSTAT only prints the lower-left triangle and the diagonal values of 1.0.

Figure 9.3
A square correlation matrix

	VIQ	PIQ	FSIQ	READ	SPELL	ARITH	AGGRESS	WITHDRAW
VIQ	1.0	.65	.91	.54	.49	.61	-.01	.26
PIQ	.65	1.0	.94	.34	.28	.52	-.03	.17
FSIQ	.91	.94	1.0	.49	.43	.62	-.01	.24
READ	.54	.34	.49	1.0	.83	.63	.14	.10
SPELL	.49	.28	.43	.83	1.0	.65	.15	.07
ARITH	.61	.52	.62	.63	.65	1.0	.03	.10
AGGRESS	-.01	-.03	-.01	.14	.15	.03	1.0	-.19
WITHDRAW	.26	.17	.24	1.0	.07	.10	-.19	1.0

4. Click **OK**.

Your output should look like Table 9.1.

Pearson correlation matrix

	VIQ	PIQ	FSIQ	READ	SPELL
VIQ	1.000				
PIQ	0.656	1.000			
FSIQ	0.914	0.904	1.000		
READ	0.542	0.344	0.493	1.000	
SPELL	0.176	0.095	0.156	0.831	1.000
ARITH	0.610	0.522	0.624	0.627	0.029
AGGRESS	-0.009	-0.029	-0.014	0.138	-0.025
WITHDRAW	0.261	0.170	0.241	0.099	-0.045

	ARITH	AGGRESS	WITHDRAW
ARITH	1.000		
AGGRESS	0.025	1.000	
WITHDRAW	0.099	-0.189	1.000

Number of observations: 200

Table 9.1
Corr output in lower-left triangular form

☞ The **Corr** output is too wide to fit in a tidy triangle in the Analysis window. The triangle is split into two sections and the second section is printed below the first.

Correlations between different variables are positioned in the off diagonal locations. For example, the correlation between FSIQ and READ is 0.493. You might want to refer back to the scatterplot created in Figure 8.2 to see what a correlation of 0.49 looks like.

If your data set has missing values you can instruct MYSTAT to ignore the case using either *pairwise* or *listwise* deletion options. These options are chosen in the **Corr** dialog box shown in Figure 9.3. These options tell MYSTAT to delete the case from the calculation. The default is to delete cases using the listwise option. Therefore, if no option or the listwise option is chosen, every case that has a missing value on any of the selected variables will be dropped from the calculation of every correlation. Using this option, every correlation is calculated using the same number of subjects. The pairwise option drops a case from a calculation only when the value is missing for one of the variables in the pair. If you choose the pairwise option, and you have missing values, two lower-left triangular matrices are produced. The first contains the correlation coefficients and the second contains whole numbers indicating the number of cases used in the calculation of each coefficient.

In chapter 8, it was stated that the Pearson coefficient measures the degree of linear association between variables. Let's do a quick demonstration of this property.

1. Load the *Powers* data.

   Powers contains fifty cases with six named variables: X, $Y1$, $Y2$, $Y3$, $Y4$, $Y5$. The X variable is simply the case number (i.e., consecutive numbers from 1–50). $Y1$ is the X variable to the first power, which means that X and $Y1$ are identical. $Y2$ is the square of the X variable, $Y3$ is the cube of the X variable, and $Y4$ and $Y5$ are the fourth and fifth powers of the X variable. If you produce separate plots of each of these Y variables with respect to the X variable (place the Y variables on the y-axis), you will note that the degree of curvature for the plots increases. For example, $Y1$ versus X is a straight line, $Y2$ versus X is slightly curved, and $Y5$ versus X is highly curved.

   Now produce all the correlations between these variables.

2. Choose the **Corr** command under the **Analyze** menu.

3. Click **OK** to have correlations calculated on all the variables in Table 9.2.

Table 9.2
Pearson correlations for the Powers data set

Pearson correlation matrix

	X	Y1	Y2	Y3	Y4
X	1.000				
Y1	1.000	1.000			
Y2	0.969	0.969	1.000		
Y3	0.919	0.919	0.986	1.000	
Y4	0.869	0.869	0.959	0.992	1.000
Y5	0.824	0.824	0.928	0.975	0.995

	Y5
Y5	1.000

Number of observations: 50

All these data points are derived directly from one another and form functional relationships. This means even though these relationships are curved, they are perfect. However, the only Pearson correlations that indicate perfect relationships are between variables that form linear scatterplots. Pearson correlations are higher between variables with closer exponents (these pairs form more linear scatterplots) and lower between variables whose exponents are further apart (these pairs form curved scatterplots). As you will see in the next section, if you want to measure associations that do not depend on an assumption of linearity, the Spearman coefficient is used.

Spearman Rank

The Spearman rank correlation is symbolized by r_s in most textbooks and it uses only rank order information. If a variable consists of the values 1, 3, 14, and 22 and was then ranked, the values would be 1, 2, 3, and 4. The Spearman correlation is simply a Pearson correlation between two variables whose values are ranked. Indeed, it can be shown that the traditional calculation formula for the Spearman correlation is equivalent to the Pearson formula when one uses two sets of consecutive untied ranks. Tied values can be replaced by averaged ranks, which is how MYSTAT computes ranks with the **Rank** command. Using the Pearson formula on ranks averaged for ties produces a Spearman correlation coefficient that has been corrected for ties.

Pearson correlations can be 1 (or –1) only if the x and y values fall on a straight line in a scatterplot. Spearman correlations can be 1 only if the ranks of the x and y values are identical, and –1 only if the ranks of x are the reverse of the ranks of y. That is, the ranks would fall on a straight line in a scatterplot of ranks.

Calculating r_s

To calculate the Spearman coefficient, rank the variable values using the **Rank** command under the **Data** menu and then calculate a Pearson correlation using **Corr** under the **Analysis** menu on the ranked data set.

To conduct this analysis with the *Powers* data:

1. Make sure the *Powers* data set is open.
2. Choose the **Rank** command under the **Data** menu.
3. Select every variable to be used in ranking, by double-clicking on them in the "Select rank variables" box.

   ☞ You will need to double-click on every variable to select it for ranking. Don't forget to scroll to select Y5.

4. Click **OK**.
5. Save the ranked data as *Powers Ranked*.
6. Open the *Powers Ranked* data.

WARNING: *If you don't use this new data set you will be computing the same Pearson coefficients found in Table 9.2.*

7. Choose **Corr** under the **Analyze** menu.
8. Click **OK** because you want to calculate correlations for all the variables.

Because all the data are in rank order, the correlations calculated are Spearman correlations even though MYSTAT labels the output as a Pearson correlation matrix (see Table 9.3). Because each of these variables formed a functional monotonic relationship with all the other variables, you should not be surprised to see the results produced in Table 9.3. While the *Powers* variables all formed functional relationships (see chapter 8), the Spearman correlation measures in addition the degree of association in monotonic statistical relationships.

Pearson correlation matrix

	X	Y1	Y2	Y3	Y4
X	1.000				
Y1	1.000	1.000			
Y2	1.000	1.000	1.000		
Y3	1.000	1.000	1.000	1.000	
Y4	1.000	1.000	1.000	1.000	1.000
Y5	1.000	1.000	1.000	1.000	1.000

Table 9.3 cont.

Table 9.3
Spearman correlations for the Powers data set

Pearson correlation matrix						
	X	Y1	Y2	Y3	Y4	Y5
Y5	1.000					

Number of observations: 50

This example points out a major similarity (use of the same formula) and a major difference (a linear versus a rank interpretation) between the two correlations.

Bivariate Regression Analysis

When you expect that two variables may be related, you might hypothesize that one of the variable's values can be used to predict the values of the second variable. This statistical procedure for prediction is called *regression analysis*, and the equation for the *best fitting* straight line is called the *linear regression equation*. Regression equations and the procedures for determining the best fit were discussed in chapter 8.

A simple example will illustrate the regression technique. Earlier you saw that the Pearson correlation between VIQ and READ scores in the *School Referrals* file was .542. You might construct the best straight line that fits the data to make predictions, and then conduct an inferential test to determine if this straight line is a significant predictor of the criterion. All of this can easily be done with the **Regress** program under the **Analyze** menu.

The Problem

You are a public school teacher and you wish to find out whether your students' verbal intelligence scores (VIQ) can predict their reading scores (READ). If the prediction is statistically significant, then you wish to construct the best equation for taking those intelligence scores and predicting how well other children can be expected to do on the same reading test.

The Solution

1. Write the null and alternative hypotheses.

In regression analysis, you are asking whether the increase in accuracy of prediction of the individual data values when using the regression equation is significantly better than predicting the data values without the equation. We will state the null and alternative hypotheses using words.

H_0: The regression equation doesn't significantly improve our predictions.

H_1: The regression equation significantly improves the predictions.

2. Set the alpha level.

Set your alpha level = .05 for this problem.

3. Collect the data.

The data are contained in the *School Referrals* file.

4. Calculate the statistic.

1. With the *School Referrals* data loaded, choose the **Regress** command under the **Analyze** menu.
2. In the "Dependent" box double-click on **READ**.

   This selects the criterion or dependent variable READ. In the "Equation:" box, READ = CONSTANT will automatically appear.
3. In the "Independent" box double-click **VIQ**.

   You have chosen the independent or predictor variable, and it will be added to the equation. The "Equation:" box should look like Figure 9.4.

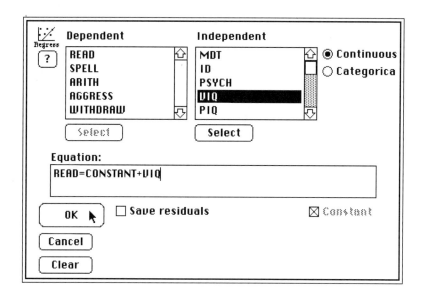

Figure 9.4
Regress dialog box

4. Click **OK**

   Look at the "Analysis of Variance" summary table at the bottom of the output. Here MYSTAT is conducting a significance test using the F statistic to determine whether the regression equation significantly improves your predictions. Do you remember your null hypothesis from step 1? All you need to consider is the reported p value (labeled P in the output). If the p value is less than the alpha level set in step 2, reject H_o.

Table 9.4
School Referrals regression results of VIQ predicting READ using the data file

Dep var: READ   N: 200   Multiple R: .542   Squared multiple R: .294
Adjusted squared multiple R: .290   Standard error of estimate: 12.318

Variable	Coefficient	Std error	Std coef	Tolerance	T	P(2 tail)
CONSTANT	42.262	5.086	0.000	.	8.309	0.000
VIQ	0.530	0.058	0.542	.100E+01	9.077	0.000

Analysis of Variance

Source	Sum-of-squares	DF	Mean-square	F-ratio	P
Regression	12502.171	1	12502.171	82.401	0.000
Residual	30041.329	198	151.724		

5. Decide whether or not to reject the null hypothesis.

Because the *p* value reported is less than .05, reject H_0.

6. Write a summary statement.

In this case the researcher might report: "For these children, verbal IQ was found to be a significant predictor of reading scores (r = .542, F = 82.4, df 1, 198, p < .005)." The generated regression equation is Expected Reading = 42.262 + 0.53VIQ. To place confidence intervals around the expected reading score the standard error of estimate of 12.318 can be used.

> In the summary statement the regression equation is in the form of $\hat{Y} = a + bX$, where $\hat{Y}$ is a predicted value, *a* is a constant, X is the predictor variable, and *b* is the regression coefficent. This is the how regression equations are typically reported.

Several other options are available in the **Regress** dialog box shown in Figure 9.4. In the top-right corner of the dialog box are two choices for the independent variable: continuous or categorical. The default choice is continuous. If an independent variable is categorical you must click the categorical option before you double-click on the independent variable. You will then be asked for the number of levels for that variable. (This is the same as choosing a factor in ANOVA which was described in chapter 7.) The levels for a categorical predictor must be coded in whole numbers starting with 1. The constant option in the lower-right corner of the dialog box allows you to construct equations in which the constant is not estimated. Regression without a constant is used very infrequently and therefore this option will seldom be used. In the lower-left portion of the dialog box is an option to save residuals. If you select the **Save residuals** box, MYSTAT creates a file containing the variables you used in your equation, the estimated criterion values (ESTIMATE), residuals (RESIDUAL), the standard error of prediction (SEPRED), leverage (LEVERAGE), Cook's D (COOK), and externally studentized residuals (STUDENT). The meanings of these variables are discussed later.

In addition to saving the file, the **Save residuals** option lists cases whose Y values are poorly predicted or whose X values are atypical. It also prints the Durbin-Watson statistic and the first-order autocorrelation coefficient. The autocorrelation coefficient measures the correlation of the residuals from case to case. The Durbin-Watson statistic tests whether the autocorrelation equals zero. These measures are important in business and economics where regression analysis is used to solve problems involving time series data. This topic is not discussed in this tutorial; however, an excellent discussion of autocorrelation and the Durbin-Watson statistic can be found in Neter, Wasserman, and Kutner (1990).

Assumptions for Regression Analysis

There are three requirements that must be met before using ordinary linear regression: the data points must be uniformly scattered around the regression line (called the *homoscedasticity of variance*), the data values must be independent of each other, and true relation between Y and X should be linear. In addition, in order for the tests of significance to appropriate, the residuals must come from a normal distribution. These assumptions are most often verified by looking at a scatterplot.

■ Multiple Regression Analysis

When several quantitative independent variables are used to estimate a single criterion score, the procedure is called *multiple regression analysis*. Instead of calculating a regression line that fits the data, you calculate a regression plane. Figure 9.5 shows a regression plane in which verbal intelligence scores (VIQ) are combined with performance IQs (PIQ) to predict the dependent variable, reading achievement scores (READ). The regression surface is no longer a line but a plane. More than two predictors can't be easily graphed because the graph would contain more than three dimensions. MYSTAT can conduct a multiple regression using any number of independent variables, but MYSTAT will not produce three-dimensional graphs. Figure 9.5 was produced using SYSTAT, a professional statistics package.

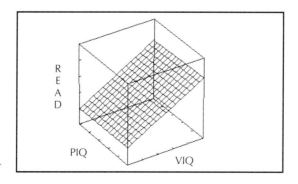

Figure 9.5
A regression plane created using SYSTAT

The Problem Assume you are interested in discovering whether VIQ and PIQ scores combine to predict READ in children. You can use the *School Referrals* data set to answer this question.

The Solution Using the following six steps conduct the multiple regression analysis:

1. **Write the null and alternative hypotheses.**

   H_o: The regression equation using both VIQ and PIQ doesn't significantly improve our predictions.

   H_1: The regression equation using both VIQ and PIQ significantly improves the predictions.

2. **Set the alpha level.**

   Set the alpha level at .05 for this problem.

3. **Collect the data.**

   1. Open the *School Referrals* data set.

4. **Calculate the statistic.**

   1. Choose the **Regress** command under the **Analyze** menu.
   2. Double-click on **READ** in the "Dependent" box.

      This selects the dependent or criterion variable.
   3. Sequentially double-click on both **VIQ** and **PIQ** in the "Independent" box.

      This selects VIQ and PIQ as independent or predictor variables.

      The "Equation" box in the **Regress** dialog box should look like Figure 9.6.

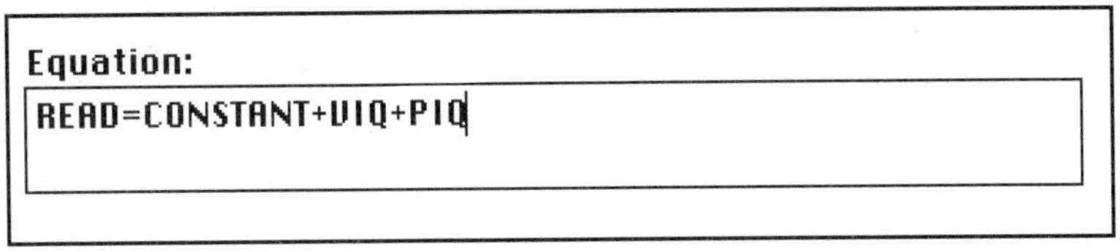

   Figure 9.6
   The "Equation" box in the **Regress** dialog box for a multiple regression

   ```
   Equation:
   READ=CONSTANT+VIQ+PIQ
   ```

   4. Click **OK**.

      Your output should be identical to Table 9.5.

Table 9.5
Multiple regression output for VIQ and PIQ predicting READ

Dep var: READ   N: 200   Multiple R: .542   Squared multiple R: .294
Adjusted squared multiple R: .287   Standard error of estimate: 12.347

Variable	Coefficient	Std error	Std coef	Tolerance	T	P(2 tail)
CONSTANT	42.882	5.627	0.000	.	7.620	0.000
VIQ	0.543	0.078	0.556	0.5697305	7.006	0.000
PIQ	-0.019	0.075	-0.021	0.5697305	-0.260	0.795

Analysis of Variance

Source	Sum-of-squares	DF	Mean-square	F-ratio	P
Regression	12512.502	2	6256.251	41.040	0.000
Residual	30030.998	197	152.442		

5. Decide whether or not to reject the null hypothesis.

Because the p value for the F reported in the ANOVA table is less than .05, reject H_0.

6. Write a summary statement.

The researcher might report: "For these children, Verbal IQ and Performance IQ scores were found to significantly predict reading scores (R = .542, F = 41.04, df = 2,197, p < .0005)." The generated regression equation is Expected Reading = 42.882 + 0.543VIQ − 0.019PIQ. To place confidence intervals around the expected reading score, the standard error of estimate (12.347) can be used.

There is a complication. The overall equation is significant, but the PIQ coefficient is not. We cannot conclude that both variables are needed to predict READ. Look back at Table 9.4. Note that the multiple correlation (.542) is the same for both models indicating that the prediction is not significantly improved by adding PIQ. At the same time, we cannot conclude that PIQ is not a good predictor of READ. Try regressing READ on PIQ instead of VIQ. The multiple correlation is .344, somewhat less than before but still significant.

Note that the correlation between VIQ and PIQ is .656. Since each variable is related to READ separately, this means that either variable is doing part of the work of the other when predicting READ. When both are put together, the stronger predictor (VIQ) is significant and the other predictor (PIQ) has no useful prediction to add independently. When this condition exists, it is difficult to make simple statements about the predictors because the relationship between them masks their separate ability to predict.

The t-test values in the upper portion of the output can be used to test whether each individual predictor is contributing to the prediction. Again, you look at these p values to make the decision. VIQ is a significant predictor, but PIQ with a p value of .795 is not. Look at how little PIQ changed the output. It would be important for parents, teachers, and psychologists to know how little a child's Performance IQ adds to VIQs when predicting some measures of academic achievement. As discussed previously, the tolerance value indicates how unique each variable in the regression is. If independent variables are not unique, they will be correlated with one another. The square of their correlation indicates how much variance they share. Look back at Table 9.1. The correlation between VIQ and PIQ is .656. If you square this value, you get .430336. This means that 43% of the variance in the predictors are shared. The unique variance of each independent variable is 1 − .430336 = .569664. How does this value agree with the tolerance figure reported in Table 9.5. The difference is due to rounding error and the number of decimals displayed in Table 9.1.

Outlier Detection

When you conduct bivariate regressions, it is a relatively simple matter to use box plots, stem-and-leaf plots, and scatter plots to detect outlying cases. With two or more predictor variables, graphic outlier detection becomes more and more problematic. With multiple regressions you need to interpret indices that detect outliers. There are three ways that outliers can be produced in data sets. The first is that the values for the predictors or independent values may be unusual. The second is when the criterion or y values are unusual. Finally, a single data point may have an undue impact on the regression equation.

Leverage

A *leverage* measure indicates whether or not the predictor values for a specific case are aberrant. The leverage value measures the distance between predictor values for any specific case and the average of the predictor values for all the cases in the study. If the leverage value is large, it indicates that the predictor values for this case are far from the mean of all the predictors.

There are several rules for using leverage values to identify outliers. (1) A leverage is often considered large if it is more than twice as large as the average leverage value. (2) Consider a leverage value greater than .5 to be large. (3) Finally, some researchers look for gaps between where most of the leverages are concentrated and a few stray leverages. The stray leverages are considered large.

Studentized Deleted Residuals

Studentized deleted residuals indicate how different predicted values are from their corresponding actual values. When the regression analysis is completed, a regression equation of the form $\hat{Y} = a + b_1 X_1 + b_2 X_2 + \ldots$ is calculated. You can calculate expected criterion values ($\hat{Y}$) for any set of predictor values by substituting the predictor scores into the regression equation. For each case both the actual criterion score (Y) and the predicted criterion score ($\hat{Y}$) are available. Using these two values, you can calculate the residual ($Y - \hat{Y}$). The residual is the amount by which the regression equation missed the actual criterion value. (See Figure 8.15 and the earlier discussion about errors and residuals.)

It is difficult to interpret the absolute value of these residuals to detect outliers for two reasons. The first is a problem of scale. If the original variables are measured with numbers whose scale is small (i.e., the numbers might vary from 1–10 with a mean of five), a residual of fifteen might be quite large. Fifteen in this example is three times the mean. However, if the variables are measured on a scale of 1 to 1000 with a mean of 500, missing the criterion by 15 points might indicate a very close approximation. The second problem with using absolute values of residuals is that if the criterion value is abnormal, it unduly influences the regression equation so that the regression line is pulled closer to the criterion value than it would be if this case were eliminated from the analysis. The interpretation problems are solved by using *Studentized deleted residuals*. Studentized deleted residuals are transformed residual scores. The transformation standardizes residuals and calculates the value without including particular cases in the analysis. Thus, studentized deleted residuals take care of both interpretation difficulties.

Studentized deleted residuals take the form of a *t* distribution. Judd and McClelland (1989) give the following advice for interpreting studentized deleted residuals:

> We can suggest an easy rule of thumb for identifying outliers. For reasonably large *n*, approximately 95% of the studentized deleted residuals (which have a *t* distribution) will be between −2 and +2. Thus, studentized deleted residuals with an absolute value less than 2 are not surprising, and we will not consider them to be unusual. However, if the absolute value of the studentized deleted residual is greater than 2, then it probably deserves another look because values that large should occur less than 5% of the time (approximately). Only about 1% of the studentized deleted residuals should be less than −3 or greater than +3. So, if the absolute value of the studentized deleted residual is greater than 3 careful attention to that observation is required. Finally, absolute values of studentized deleted residuals greater than 4 ought to be extremely rare; if the absolute value is greater than 4, then all alarm bells ought to sound (p. 225).

Cook's D

Cook's D measures the influence a case has on the regression. If you eliminate one case from a regression analysis and recompute the results, the value of the regression coefficients should not change dramatically. If that case has undue influence on the regression equation, then removing that case dramatically changes the values of the computed regression coefficients. Cook's D measures this influence.

Again, we use several rules to determine when Cook's D is too large. One rule is to consider any value greater than one or two as atypical. Another rule is to look for gaps between the small Cook's D values and the larger ones. Finally, according to Judd and McClelland (1989), a frequent rule is to consider Cook's D values large if they are greater than 4/ (Number of predictor variables + 1) * (number of subjects). If the *School Referrals* data is used with VIQ predicting READ, then values above 4/(2)*(200) = .01 would be considered large.

MYSTAT flags unusual cases, using approximate 99% confidence intervals on Cook's D leverage and studentized residuals, if the **Save residuals** option is checked in the **regression** dialog box. Neter, Wasserman, and Kutner (1990) and Judd and McClelland (1989) provide excellent discussions about outlier detection.

Rerun the regression in which you predict READ scores given VIQ with the **Save residuals** option chosen. The output from this analysis (in Table 9.6) details which cases are possible outliers and why MYSTAT believes they may be outliers.

Dep var: READ   N: 200   Multiple R: .542   Squared multiple R: .294
Adjusted squared multiple R: .290   Standard error of estimate: 12.318

Variable	Coefficient	Std error	Std coef	Tolerance	T	P(2 tail)
CONSTANT	42.262	5.086	0.000	.	8.309	0.000
VIQ	0.530	0.058	0.542	.100E+01	9.077	0.000

Analysis of Variance

Source	Sum-of-squares	DF	Mean-square	F-ratio	P
Regression	12502.171	1	12502.171	82.401	0.000
Residual	30041.329	198	151.724		

Warning: case 5 has undue influence (leverage = .042)
Warning: case 32 has undue influence (leverage = .042)
Warning: case 63 has undue influence (leverage = .039)
Warning: case 169 has undue influence (leverage = .034)
Warning: case 182 has undue influence (leverage = .041)
Warning: case 182 is an outlier (studentized residual = 4.456)
Warning: case 199 is an outlier (studentized residual = 3.891)
Durbin-Watson D statistic   1.961
First order autocorrelation   .018

Table 9.6
Regress output of VIQ predicting READ with the **Save residuals** option selected

You may want to investigate the *School Referrals Residuals* file, which was created to look at the variables saved from this analysis. Figure 9.7 contains the first several variables for the initial ten cases.

	ESTIMATE	RESIDUAL	LEVERAGE	COOK	STUDENT
1	87.297	-3.297	.005	0.000	-.268
2	94.185	-1.185	.008	0.000	-.096
3	86.767	-14.767	.005	.004	-1.203
4	76.700	-17.700	.015	.016	-1.452
5	66.104	-4.104	.042	.003	-.340
6	91.006	-15.006	.006	.004	-1.223
7	84.648	3.352	.005	0.000	.272
8	76.171	24.829	.016	.033	2.048
9	96.834	-19.834	.012	.015	-1.626
10	91.006	4.994	.006	0.000	.406

Figure 9.7
The *School Referrals Residuals* file

The first variable, ESTIMATE, is the estimated criterion scores ($\hat{Y}$). The second variable, RESIDUAL, contains the untransformed residual scores ($Y - \hat{Y}$). LEVERAGE and COOK's D values next are reported followed by studentized deleted residuals, STUDENT. The final three variables, which are not visible in the figure, are the standard error of prediction (SEPRED) and the criterion and predictor values (READ and VIQ).

You may wish to make influence plots using the *School Referrals* data file and compare the size of the dots with Cook's D in this file. Use the scatterplot brushing tools to investigate these cases. Remember that in chapter 7 you visually identified case 182 as an outlier.

Exercises

1. In chapter 8, you were asked to plot sextant Dip corrections (DIP) on the y-axis against the height of eye (HEIGHT) variable on the x-axis using the file *Dips*. You then rank ordered DIP, saved this file as *Dips Ranked*, and replotted the variables. Finally, you rank ordered HEIGHT in the *Dips Ranked* file and called the new file *Dips Ranked Ranked*. In this last file, both variables were rank ordered. You then plotted both ranked variables. In the first plot, you noted that the data formed a smooth curve. In the second plot, the curve was more pronounced. In the final plot you produced a straight line. Calculate the Pearson correlations between the two variables in all three data sets.

    r_{xy} for *Dips* _____

    r_{xy} for *Dips Ranked* _____

    r_{xy} for *Dips Ranked Ranked* _____

    Why does the value of the correlation change? If another student says your correlation analysis is inappropriate because these files contain variables with functional relationships, how will you reply?

2. In the file *Forecast*, are the names of sixteen world cities (CITY$), their recorded high temperatures on July 18, 1991 (RECORDED), and their projected high temperatures for July 19 (PROJECT). What is the correlation between the temperature measured in a city on one day and the projected temperature for that same city on the following day?

3. Conduct a bivariate regression in which you use VIQ to predict ARITH using the *School Referrals* data set. Write a summary statement.

4. Are any outliers identified in the analysis in exercise 3? Write down the case numbers and the MYSTAT indicators if present.

5. Produce a scatterplot with the regression equation for exercise 3.

6. Using the generated regression equation, what would be the expected arithmetic score for a child with a VIQ of 128?

7. In a previous exercise you produced a file titled *School Referrals Deleted* in which you dropped high and low FSIQ scores. Run a regression analysis using this data set in which FSIQ is used to predict READ. Compare these results with those you produced with the full data set earlier. Why are there differences?

8. Use the *States* file to conduct a bivariate regression in which you use winter temperatures to predict population densities. Is there a significant regression equation? Write a summary statement for this experiment.
9. The *Karachi* file was introduced in chapter 7. Calculate the correlation between the variables BACTERIA, LEAD, ARSENIC, CADMIUM, and CYANIDE. Lead is almost universally present in the food. In only twelve samples was no lead found. Eight of those twelve samples were bottled colas. However, arsenic, cadmium, and cyanide are not universally found. When one of these three ingredients is found, how frequently do the other two occur? Some of these correlations are conducted with one or both of the variables measured dichotomously. What might be another name for the correlations?

Notes

[1] In the top line of output, MYSTAT lists the dependent variable (Dep var:) as READ, with 200 cases. Directly to the right, you will see the value .542 labeled "Multiple R." The **Regress** program works for multiple regressions as well as bivariate regressions. In multiple regressions the correlation is calculated using several predictors and is called a *multiple R* instead of a simple Pearson correlation (r). However, in this case, because we are only analyzing one predictor, the listing for "Multiple R" is the same as the Pearson r that you found (look at Table 9.1 where VIQ and READ intersect). At the end of this first line, the correlation is squared and labeled "Squared multiple R" with a value of .294. In some textbooks this is called the *coefficient of determination*. The coefficient of determination tells you the percent of variance in the dependent variable, READ in this case, accounted for by the predictor variable, VIQ in this case. This value is then adjusted and labeled in second line as the "Adjusted squared multiple R", which value equals .290. This adjusted squared multiple R indicates the percentage of variance that the regression equation would account for if it were used to predict for cases in the population from which this data set was sampled. Next, the "Standard error of estimate" is reported. The standard error of estimate is 12.318, which is the standard deviation of the errors in the prediction. Look back at Figure 8.15. The distance that the regression equation misses the dots is called the *residual*. The standard error of estimate is the standard deviation of these residuals.

The middle section of the output details the regression equation and some associated statistics. Looking under "Coefficient", you will note that the constant is 42.262 and the VIQ is 0.53. Again, referring back to chapter 8, where you learned that MYSTAT reports the regression equation using the general equation of $y = a + bx$, the constant is the a value and the VIQ coefficient is the b value or slope in the regression equation. These values are also known as *regression coefficients*. If you want to predict another child's READ score and you know his or her VIQ, the following equation is best: READ = 42.262 + 0.530(VIQ). If a child has a VIQ of 90, the expected READ score is 89.962.

The symbols used for regression lines change from text to text. In this tutorial a straight line equation will be represented by the general equation $y = a + bx$. In some texts this equation is written $y = bx + c$ or $y = mx + b$. Don't let the changes in abbreviations confuse you. Also, since a regression equation produces expected scores, the general form for the regression equation in this tutorial is $\hat{Y} = aX + b$. The $\hat{Y}$ value indicates a predicted score.

In the next column are the standard errors (predicted Std error) of the coefficients. In the following column are the standard coefficients, labeled "Std coef". These values are used in a regression equation when all the data values are turned into standard scores by subtracting the mean of each variable from the variable's value and dividing that difference by the standard deviation of the variable. Scores produced by this procedure are called Z scores and typically have means of zero and standard deviations of one. Note that the constant disappears (it's value becomes zero), and for bivariate regressions the standardized coefficient for the predictor is the Pearson correlation. In some texts these standardized coefficients are called *beta weights*.

Next to the standardized coefficients are tolerance values. The tolerance value is only useful in multiple regressions. It is a measure of the uniqueness of each predictor in the regression problem. Since there is only a single predictor in a bivariate regression (VIQ), it is unique and always has a tolerance value of 1.0 (this value is written in scientific notation in Table 9.4). The t values in the last column are inferential tests (t-tests) that determine if the coefficients for the constant and predictors are different than zero. Rarely will the constant ever be tested, so that t value is infrequently used. In a bivariate regression there is only one predictor and the t value reported is simply the square root of the F value reported in the "Analysis of Variance" table at the bottom. In bivariate regression, both the t and the F value give the same information.

10

An Introduction to Analysis of Covariance

In chapter 7, we discussed analysis of variance (ANOVA) techniques. ANOVA is used to compare the means of more than two groups, and the effect of the categorical variable on the values of the dependent variable is evaluated. In chapter 9, we discussed correlation and regression techniques which evaluate the effect of one or more continuous independent variables on the values of a single continuous dependent variable. In this chapter, we will merge the two techniques. We will analyze data that contain both categorical and continuous independent variables, and we will separate the effects of these different varieties of independent variable. This analysis technique is called *analysis of covariance,* or *ANCOVA*. While analysis of covariance (ANCOVA) is sporadically covered in beginning courses, understanding the general idea behind ANCOVA and its ability to increase the power of your statistical decisions is important.

Objectives

At the end of this tutorial you should be able to
- Decide when to use ANCOVA
- Discuss the two major uses of ANCOVA
- Acknowledge which of those uses is more often justified
- Direct MYSTAT to conduct ANCOVA

■ Determining Whether ANCOVA Is Appropriate

With ANCOVA techniques, unlike ANOVA or regression techniques, you have two different types of independent variables. At least one categorical and one continuous independent variable are present.

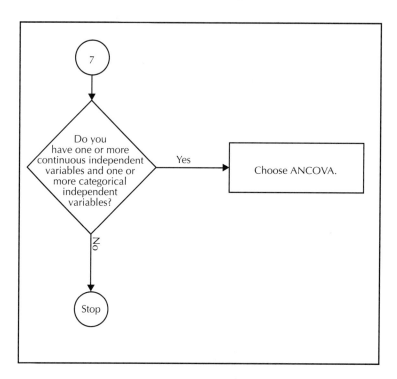

Figure 10.1
Decision model for ANCOVA

■ What Is ANCOVA?

Analysis of covariance, or ANCOVA, is a combination of regression and ANOVA techniques. In ANCOVA, a continuous independent variable is called a *covariate* and a categorical independent variable is called a *factor*. Usually the covariate is used in a regression analysis to correct or adjust the dependent scores and then a regular analysis of variance is conducted using these corrected scores. Under certain circumstances researchers gained a great deal of power using these analyses. (Remember, the power of a statistical test is its ability to detect differences in the dependent variable.)

ANCOVA (indeed even ANOVA) is also taught as an elaboration of regression analysis in which both continuous and categorical predictors are used. Using this approach, it is logical for a researcher to be interested in the effects of the continuous variable while controlling for the effects of the categorical variable. This ANCOVA approach is often used in research investigating bias (for example, to tell whether a test is biased by race or sex, whether an employer discriminates by age, and so on).

In ANCOVA, the covariate may be included in the design for two purposes. The first purpose is to statistically equate groups that are not similar. There are real problems with this practice, and almost all textbooks caution against using ANCOVA for group adjustment. When reading papers in which ANCOVA is used for this purpose, you should interpret the results with caution. The reasons for these interpretation difficulties are beyond the scope of this tutorial, but they are discussed in detail in advanced statistics texts.

The second purpose for using ANCOVA is to increase the power of the statistical analysis. If there is a covariate (continuous variable) unrelated to the grouping condition (categorical variable) but related to the dependent variable, including the covariate in the analysis may dramatically increase the power of the statistical test. This is easily accomplished if the investigator can randomly assign subjects to different treatment groups.

For example, if you are a teacher interested in how a new reading curriculum affects reading scores, you might give the children a reading pretest (the covariate), randomly assign the children to different treatment groups, and after using the new curriculum give a reading posttest. The reading pretest and posttest scores will be related. You expect children with high scores on the reading pretest to have high scores on the reading posttest and children with low scores on the reading pretest to have low scores on the reading posttest. There is a correlation between the level at which children read today and the level at which they read in the future. In chapter 9, you learned that the square of the correlation coefficient (the coefficient of determination) indicates how much variance in the dependent variable is accounted for by the predictor variable. By using the pretest results to predict the posttest results, some of the variance in the dependent variable can be accounted for. Because the covariate (pretest) and the grouping variable (factor) have no relationship to each other, the variance accounted for in the dependent variable by the covariate will have no relationship to the categorical independent variable. Remember from chapter 7 that variance not related to the treatment is error variance. Therefore, if the variance in the dependent variable accounted for by the covariate is statistically removed, you decrease the error variance. Also, since the error variance is in the denominator of the F statistic, if you decrease the denominator of a fraction, the value of the fraction increases. Therefore by including a covariate, you will increase the value of the fraction (the F value). The only problem is that you lose one degree of freedom for the covariate. So the amount of error variance removed by the covariate must compensate for the degree of freedom lost. Following is an example that illustrates the increase in power one may get using ANCOVA instead of ANOVA.

The Problem

You are the research coordinator for the American Nursing Association. You are interested in a new approach to teaching surgical assistance in a cardiac valve replacement. You give the nurses a pretest on their knowledge of this material (PRETEST). They are randomly assigned to two different curricular approaches (CURRICUL) and to two different instructors (TEACHER). After instruction, you give a posttest. You want to find out whether the curriculum, the teacher, or a combination (this is called an *interaction*) makes a difference in the posttest scores. These data are stored in the *Cardiac* file on your data disk.

The ANOVA Solution

The ANOVA results for this problem are presented first. These results will then be compared to the ANCOVA results. To analyze the *Cardiac* data using ANOVA, you want to detect whether there are differences in the dependent variable (POSTTEST) using the categorical variables CURRICUL and TEACHER. Each independent variable has two different levels. You will be conducting a 2 x 2 ANOVA.

Use the same six-step solution that you used to solve the *Schizophrenia* problem on pages 103 through 105 in chapter 7, but to calculate the statistic follow these directions:

1. Load the *Cardiac file.*
2. Choose **ANOVA** under the **Analyze** menu.
3. Double-click on **POSTTEST** in the "Dependent" box.
4. Double-click on **CURRICUL** in the "Factor(s)" box.
5. Type **2** when asked for the number of levels, and click **OK**.
6. Double-click on **TEACHER** in the "Factor(s)" box.
7. Type **2** when asked for the number of levels, and click **OK**.

Your completed ANOVA dialog box should look like Figure 10.2.

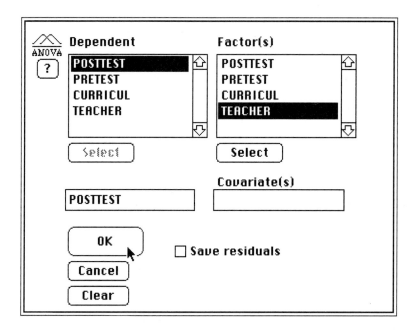

Figure 10.2
Completed ANOVA dialog box for the *Cardiac* data

8. Click **OK**.

   Your results should look like those presented in Table 10.1

Table 10.1 ANOVA results for the *Cardiac* data

Dep var: POSTTEST   N: 40   Multiple R: .646   Squared multiple R: .417

Analysis of Variance

Source	Sum-of-squares	DF	Mean-square	F-ratio	P
CURRICUL	422.500	1	422.500	21.423	0.000
TEACHER	22.500	1	22.500	1.141	0.293
CURRICUL*TEACHER	62.500	1	62.500	3.169	0.083
Error	710.000	36	19.722		

If the alpha level is set at .05, there is one significant finding using ANOVA. The curriculum does make a difference in the nurses scores. Note that the error sum of squares is 710 with 36 degrees of freedom, providing a mean-square error of 19.722.

The ANCOVA Solution

With ANCOVA, you use the covariate (PRETEST), which is unrelated to the categorical independent variables (CURRICUL and TEACHER). The covariate is used to reduce the sum-of-squares error term. As mentioned earlier, one degree of freedom will be used by the covariate, so the sum-of-squares accounted for by the covariate must be worth the degree of freedom lost to the error term. Remember from chapter 7 that if you divide the sum-of-squares by the degrees of freedom (DF) you will obtain the mean-square value. If the mean-square error is made smaller, the F statistic will be larger, and the power of the test will be increased.

You will use the six-step in the solution.

1. State the null and alternative hypotheses.

In ANCOVA there may be several sets of null and alternative hypotheses. In this problem, you will have a null and alternative hypothesis for each of the independent variables (both continuous and categorical) and for the interaction between the categorical predictors. ANCOVA hypotheses are stated without out symbols.

H_{o1}: There is no curricular effect on posttest scores.
H_{11}: H_{o1} is false.
H_{o2}: There is no teacher effect on posttest scores.
H_{12}: H_{o2} is false.
H_{o3}: There is no interaction effect between curriculum and teacher on posttest scores.
H_{13}: H_{o3} is false.

Notice that these are the same hypotheses as in the ANOVA. We are using ANCOVA to increase the power of each of these tests.

2. Set the alpha level.

We'll use the same alpha level as we did for the ANOVA solution, .05.

3. Collect the data.

The data for this problem are found in the file *Cardiac*.

1. Open the *Cardiac* file on the data disk. (If *Cardiac* is still loaded, simply click in the Data Editor to make it the active window.)

   When you open the file you will note that there is a variable for the pretest (PRETEST), which is the covariate or continuous independent variable. The dependent variable is POSTTEST, and the two variables for the curriculum type (CURRICUL) and the teacher (TEACHER) are the categorical independent variables.

4. Calculate the statistic.

1. Select the **ANOVA** command under the **Analyze** menu. The ANOVA dialog box appears.
2. Double-click on **POSTTEST** in the "Dependent" box to choose POSTTEST as the dependent variable.
3. Double-click on **CURRICUL** in the "Factor(s)" box to select CURRICUL as the first categorical independent variable.
4. Type **2** when asked for the number of levels in the second and click **OK**. This indicates that there are two types of curriculums in this experiment.
5. Double-click on **TEACHER** in the "Factor(s)" box to select TEACHER as the second categorical independent variable.
6. Type **2** when asked for the number of levels for this factor and click **OK**. This indicates that there are two teachers in this experiment.

   You should now be looking at the first dialog box on the computer screen. So far, you have done exactly what you did for the two-way ANOVA. The next step makes this an ANCOVA.

7. Click once in the "Covariate(s)" box and type **PRETEST**.

   You are telling MYSTAT that the pretest values are to be used as the continuous independent variable, or the covariate.

   WARNING: *You have to type the word* **PRETEST** *into the "Covariate(s)" box. You cannot double-click to enter variables into this box.*

   The completed ANCOVA dialog box should look like Figure 10.3.

What Is ANCOVA?

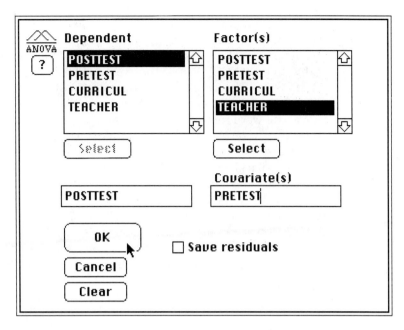

Figure 10.3
Completed ANCOVA dialog box for the *Cardiac* data

8. Click **OK**.

The ANCOVA output is shown in Table 10.2.

Dep var: POSTTEST   N: 40   Multiple R: .845   Squared multiple R: .714

Table 10.2
ANCOVA results for the *Cardiac* data

Analysis of Variance

Source	Sum-of-squares	DF	Mean-square	F-ratio	P
CURRICUL	422.500	1	422.500	42.484	0.000
TEACHER	22.500	1	22.500	2.262	0.142
CURRICUL* TEACHER	62.500	1	62.500	6.285	0.017
PRETEST	361.929	1	361.929	36.394	0.000
Error	348.071	35	9.945		

In the ANCOVA results, the interaction (CURRICULUM * TEACHER) is significant, p = 0.017. This indicates that the curriculum and the teacher together affect the dependent variable when the pretest is controlled. When a single categorical independent variable is referred to in either ANOVA or ANCOVA, it is sometimes referred to as a *main effect* to distinguish it from interactions. The first main effect, CURRICUL, is significant (p = 0.000). The second main effect, TEACHER, is nonsignificant (p = 0.142). Finally the pretest is a significant predictor (or covariate) of the scores ($p \leq 0.0005$), although this statistical significance is not necessary for the ANCOVA to be valid, and it is not one of our hypotheses.

WARNING: *With a significant interaction you should be careful about interpreting significant main effects.*

Let's compare the two summary tables starting with the Error line. In the ANOVA table, the error sum-of-squares is 710, while in the ANCOVA table, the error sum-of-squares is 348.071. The ANCOVA error sum-of-squares is smaller. Why? In the ANCOVA table there is an extra line for the effect of the covariate (PRETEST). The covariate accounts for 361.929 sum-of-squares. If you add 348.071 and 361.929 together, the result is 710. The sum-of-squares due to the covariate were removed from the ANOVA error term. The degrees of freedom for the error term in ANOVA are 36, giving a mean-square of 19.722. In ANCOVA the degrees of freedom are 35 (you lost one for the covariate), but the mean-square is 9.945, which is considerably smaller than in the ANOVA results. Now look at the curriculum by teacher interaction (CURRICUL*TEACHER). In both the ANOVA and ANCOVA tables, sum-of-squares accounted for by the interaction is 62.5. In both Table 10.1 and Table 10.2, the degrees of freedom for the interaction are 1 and the mean-square is 62.5. In the ANOVA table, the F value for the interaction is 3.169, which is nonsignificant (p = 0.083). In the ANCOVA table, the F value is 6.285. This value is considerably larger because the F value is found by dividing the mean-square of the source by the mean-square error. Since the mean-square error is reduced in ANCOVA, the F value is larger and the test is more powerful. In ANCOVA, the interaction is significant. Because of its lack of power, the ANOVA procedure was unable to detect this interaction.

This example clearly demonstrates the increase in statistical power available using ANCOVA procedures. Notice how all the other main effect F values have increased.

5. Decide whether or not to reject the hull hypothesis.

In this case you would reject the first, third, and fourth null hypotheses and fail to reject the second.

6. Write a summary statement.

For this problem, the researcher might report: "The curriculums made a difference in the nurses' scores on the cardiac valve replacement exam (F = 42.484, df = 1, 35, p = 0.000). There was no significant difference in the test scores, which were dependent upon which teacher the students had (F = 2.262, df = 1, 35, p = 0.142). However, there was a significant curriculum by teacher interaction (F = 6.285, df = 1,35 p = 0.017). Finally, the relationship between the pretest and posttest scores was significant controlling for both curriculum and teacher effects (F = 36.394, df = 1,35, p ≤ 0.0005)."

> ☞ The ANCOVA summary table (Table 10.2) is still called an analysis of variance table. You might want to output these results to the Analysis window and change the title to Analysis of Covariance before printing the results.

■ Assumptions of ANCOVA

ANCOVA has assumptions which are similar to those for ANOVA. The residuals are supposed to be random samples from a population of errors which are normally distributed with the same variance in every group and a mean of zero in every group. You can save and examine the residuals to see how plausible these assumptions are for your data.

There is an additional set of assumptions which is especially important for ANCOVA, however. Since we are making a common adjustment for all groups, the covariate should be related linearly to the dependent measure in the same way for every group. Thus, for example, if we plotted a scatterplot between POSTTEST and PRETEST for every group, all four scatterplots should look similar and the regression lines predicting POSTTEST from PRETEST should have similar slopes. This is often called the "homogeneity of slopes" assumption.

Exercises

1. Conduct an ANCOVA using the *School Referrals* data. Use MDT as the independent variable (factor), READ scores as the dependent variable, and VIQ as the covariate. If there is a group that is reading disabled, it should have significantly different scores on the reading test than other groups. Reading disabled children are supposed to be underachieving in reading. This difference should show when verbal intelligence is used as a covariate. Write a summary statement. You will need to delete MDT group 7, as there is only a single subject in this group. A group can't be formed using a single case because the variance in the group is zero. Without group 7 there are 6 remaining groups.

2. Use the *States* data. In chapter 6, exercise 3, you created a variable that separated the eastern states from the western states. Determine whether there are significant differences between the population densities of these two groups using winter temperature as a covariate. Write a summary statement for your results.

3. Use data listed in your text or assigned by your instructor. Conduct the ANCOVA and write summary statements.

11

Nonparametric Statistical Tests

Until now, we have discussed and learned how to calculate *parametric statistics*. In parametric statistics, the symbols used when writing the null and alternative hypotheses are population parameters. These parameters completely specified the location and shape of a normal distribution.

Nonparametric statistics are often termed distribution free tests. They do not assume that a population distribution must be specified by parameters. Consequently, these procedures do not use population parameters in their null or alternative hypotheses.

A complete discussion of nonparametric statistics is beyond the scope of this book. Additional information on nonparametric statistics can be found in S. Siegel (1956), and L. A. Marascuilo and M. McSweeney (1977).

Objectives

After completing this tutorial you will be able to
- Determine which nonparametric procedure is appropriate
- Calculate a one-way chi-square
- Calculate a two-way chi-square
- Calculate a Sign test
- Calculate the Wilcoxon signed-rank test
- Calculate the Friedman nonparametric analysis of variance

■ Determining Which Nonparametric Procedure to Use

You use the *one-way chi-square* test when both the independent and dependent variables are categorical. Use this statistic when you have a single independent variable and you want to compare the number of times (frequency) a category or group defined by the independent variable occurs with the number of times you expect it to occur. Usually, the expected frequencies are equal for each group, so this statistic evaluates whether the frequencies for the groups are different.

You use *two-way chi-square* tests when there are two independent categorical variables and a single categorical dependent variable. Like the one-way chi-square, the two-way chi-square determines whether the number of times a category occurs is different than what is expected. When the expected frequencies in a two-way chi-square are determined, it is assumed that the two independent variables are unrelated. Therefore, if the observed frequencies for the groups are different than the expected frequencies, there is a relationship between the independent variables.

The *Sign* test is the nonparametric equivalent of the dependent *t*-test (see chapter 6). The independent variable is categorical and consists of two levels like the dependent *t*-test. The dependent variable is assumed to be continuous, but it can't be measured using a continuous scale, so a categorical scale is substituted. This often happens when an appropriate test is unavailable, but an observer can count when the dependent variable takes one of two values (usually present or absent). The Sign test is inappropriate if the dependent variable has more than two values. Variables that take only two different values are called *binary* variables. Using the Sign test you want to know if there are differences between the two groups on the binary variable.

The *Wilcoxon* test is also a nonparametric alternative to the dependent *t*-test. The independent variable is categorical and has two levels. The dependent variable is categorical, but the dependent variable values have an order. The numbers indicate a quantity, but you only know if a case has more or less of the variable, not how much more or less. Positions in a race are good examples of this type of variable. If you know that Marsha took first place (1), Mary took second place (2), and Maria took third (3), you know that Marsha did better than Mary, but you don't know how much better. The race may have required a photo finish or Marsha may have lapped Mary. You also know that Mary did better than Maria. This test is sometimes called the *Wilcoxon signed ranks test*—the dependent variable is a rank. You want to know if there is a difference in the ranks on the dependent variable between the two related groups.

If you measure a subject two or more times, you are doing a *repeated measures analysis*. You use the *Friedman analysis of variance* test if you have a categorical independent variable (there may be more than one independent variable and each independent variable may have more than two levels) and a rank-order dependent variable that is measured more than twice. Use this test to determine whether the dependent variable differs across the groups formed by the independent variable(s).

Figure 11.1 illustrates the decision model for choosing among these nonparametric tests.

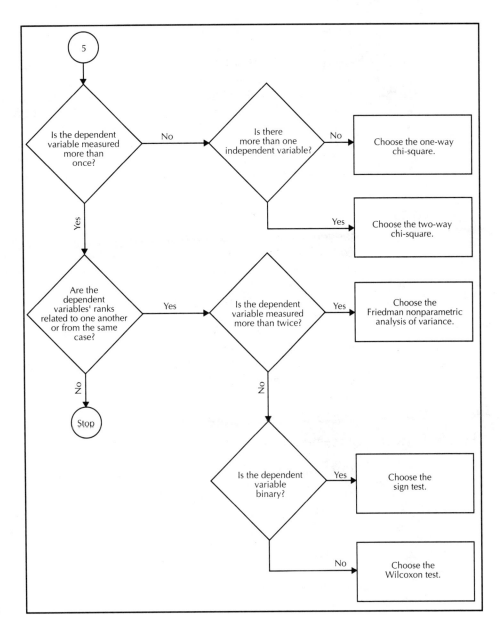

Figure 11.1
Decision model for nonparametric tests

■ One-way Chi-Square

As noted, a one-way or one-variable chi-square (χ^2) test (also called the *goodness-of-fit test*) compares a set of observed frequencies (O) with an expected set of frequencies (E). The observed frequencies for each group are the number of sample cases in each group. The expected frequencies are the number of cases you expect each group to have given the sample size. Expected frequencies are determined in two ways. First, you might have a theoretical reason to expect a certain percentage of the frequencies to be in a particular category. For example, genetic theories for dominant and recessive traits lead researchers to conclude that if the theory is correct, a certain percentage of offspring should have the dominant trait while the remainder would possess the recessive trait. Second, in the absence of a theoretical expectation, you expect random assignment to the categories. This is the procedure MYSTAT uses to assign expected frequencies. Using random assignment, each category is expected to have the same number of frequencies. If the observed frequencies are distributed differently from the expected frequencies, the population distributions for the groups are presumed to be different.

The Problem

You are a market researcher trying to decide which of four packages created for your client's product is best. You present the four different packages to 100 consumers and ask them to make a choice concerning which packaging they prefer. You code each subject with a 1 if they choose package #1, a 2 if they choose package #2, and so on. If there are no differences in preference for the four packages, you assume that each package receives an equal number of choices. Twenty-five people would choose package #1 as best, twenty-five people would choose package #2 as best, twenty-five people would choose package #3 as best, and twenty-five people would choose package #4 as best. Twenty-five is the expected frequency for each group (E). To compare the observed frequencies (O) with the expected frequencies (E), you calculate a chi-square statistic.

The Solution

As before, use six steps.

1. Write the null and alternative hypotheses.

The null hypothesis in chi-square states that the distribution of observed frequencies is identical to the distribution of expected frequencies.

$H_o: O = E$

$H_1: O \neq E$

2. Set the alpha level.

We'll choose .05.

3. Collect the data.

The data for this problem are found in the file *Package Marketing*. When you open the data set you will note that there is a single variable **CHOICE** that indicates which of the four packages was preferred.

4. Calculate the statistic.

To generate the information necessary to calculate the chi-square, do the following:

1. Select the **Tables** command under the **Analyze** menu. You will see the dialog box in Figure 11.2.

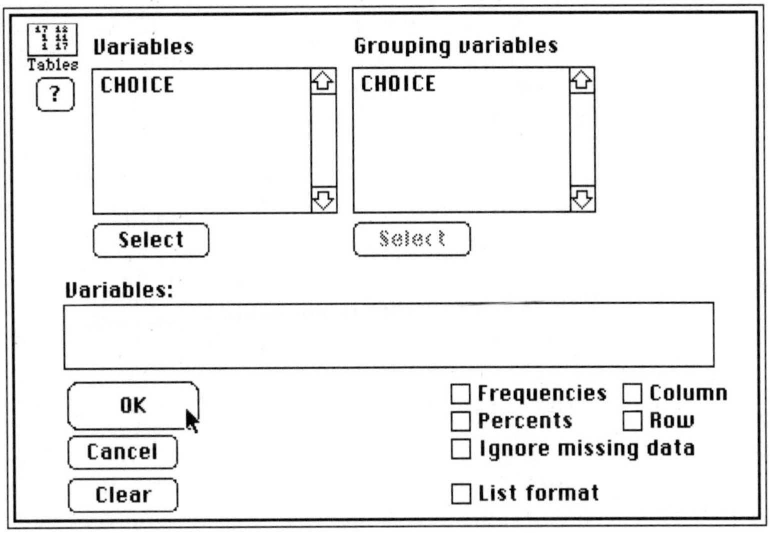

Figure 11.2 Tables dialog box

The **Tables** command produces a table of observed frequencies for each numeric variable in the data. The variables for which these tables are produced are selected by double-clicking on them in the "Variables" box. The other options in this dialog box are discussed in the two-way chi-square discussion. If a variable is not selected in the "Variables" box, MYSTAT produces tables for every numeric variable in the data.

2. Since there is only one variable in the data, click **OK**.

Table 11.1 indicates that there were nine people who indicated they preferred package #1, fifty-eight who preferred package #2, nineteen who preferred the third package, and fourteen who preferred package #4.

Table 11.1 Tabular results for the CHOICE variable

Table of values for CHOICE
Frequencies

1.000	2.000	3.000	4.000	TOTAL
9	58	19	14	100

Test statistic	Value	DF	Prob
Pearson chi-square	60.080	3	0.000
Likelihood ratio chi-square	52.569	3	0.000

MYSTAT prints the Pearson chi-square below the table, assuming equal expected frequencies for each package. The formula for a chi-square is

$$\chi^2 = \sum_{cells} \frac{(O-E)^2}{E}.$$

The $\sum$ stands for "add what follows." Cells is used as a subscript to remind you to add what follows for all the cells or groups defined by the independent variable. In many textbooks you will find subscripts and superscripts around the summation sign that indicate that you add together each of the values found for each group. In this case, there are four groups or cells, one for each preferred package. Remembering that for each of the cells the expected frequency (E) is 100/4 = 25, you will take each observed frequency (found in Table 11.1), subtract 25 from that value, square the result, divide by 25, and add the values generated for each cell together to calculate the chi-square.

Your calculated χ^2 value = 60.08, which is what MYSTAT prints.

5. Decide whether or not to reject the null hypothesis.

The critical value for chi-square marks the boundaries for rejecting the null hypothesis similar to the critical z value discussed in chapter 5. Unlike the z critical values, χ^2 critical values change for different degrees of freedom. If your obtained χ^2 is larger than the critical χ^2, then you reject the null hypothesis. Figure 11.3 illustrates this decision.

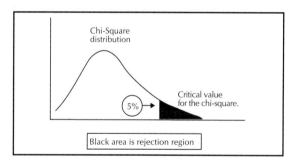

Figure 11.3
Critical χ^2 values

In this case you reject the null hypothesis. Your calculated χ^2 value of 60.08 has a $p > .0005$ as shown in Table 11.1

6. Write a summary statement.

For this problem, the researcher might report: "The different packages were not equally preferred. Subjects showed a clear preference for package #2 (χ^2 = 60.08, df = 2, p < .0005)."

Two-way Chi-Square

Another name for the two-way chi-square is the *chi-square test of independence*. When the dependent variable is measured at the categorical level and the researcher has an experimental situation with two independent variables, each with at least two categories, the two-way chi-square test is appropriate.

The Problem

You are a researcher for the Department of Defense interested in determining whether there is a relationship between the social class of military volunteers and the branch of service for which they volunteer. You collect data for a random sample of 100 recruits. The two variables are CHOICE (Army = 1, Navy = 2, Air Force = 3, and Marines = 4), and STATUS (upper class = 1, middle class = 2, lower class = 3).

The Solution

1. State the null and alternative hypotheses.

More often than not you will see this test's null and alternative hypotheses stated without symbols:

H_0: There is no relationship between the branch of service and the social class of military recruits.

H_1: There is a relationship between the branch of service and the social class of military recruits.

Obviously, the null and alternative hypothesis could be stated symbolically as was done for the goodness-of-fit test.

H_0: O = E

H_1: O ≠ E

2. Set the alpha level.

Set the alpha level to .05 again. MYSTAT will calculate the chi-square statistic, its probability, and other associated values.

3. Collect the data.

The data for this problem are found in the file *Military*.

4. Calculate the statistic.

1. Select the **Tables** command under the **Analyze** menu.

   You will receive the same dialog box as in the previous problem.

2. Double-click on **CHOICE** in the "Variables" box.

   This step selects CHOICE as one of the variables to use in constructing the table.

3. Double-click on **STATUS** in the "Grouping variables" box.

This step selects STATUS as the second variable to use in constructing the table. Since STATUS was chosen in the "Grouping variables" box, only one table will be created using both variables. If STATUS had been chosen in the "Variables" box, then two tables would be constructed, one for the different levels of CHOICE and the second for the different levels of STATUS. The bottom "Variables" box in which the model equation is written should look like Figure 11.4.

Figure 11.4
The **Tables** dialog box model for producing a two-way chi-square test

```
Variables:
CHOICE * STATUS
```

Note the asterisk in the "Variables" box, which indicates that the groups are formed by crossing the two variables. When the two variables are crossed, the groups formed are sometimes referred to as cells. For example, if the first variable, has four different values (levels) and the second variable has three different values, twelve groups or cells will be formed. The table size has a size of 4 x 3. This is illustrated in Figure 11.5.

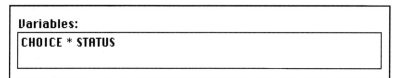

		Three levels of the second variable		
		1.000	2.000	3.000
	1.000	cell 1	cell 2	cell 3
Four levels of the first variable	2.000	cell 4	cell 5	cell 6
	3.000	cell 7	cell 8	cell 9
	4.000	cell 10	cell 11	cell 12

Figure 11.5
A table of size 4 x 3

4. Click **OK**.

You should see the output shown in Table 11.2.

5. Decide whether or not to reject the null hypothesis.

MYSTAT automatically provides the table and calculates two different chi-square statistics. The likelihood ratio chi-square is an alternative to the more familiar Pearson chi-square and is used in log-linear analyses. Log-linear analyses are beyond the scope of this book. The information you need to reject the null hypothesis is contained in the Pearson chi-square row. In this case you reject the null hypothesis. Your calculated χ^2 of 22.48 has a probability of .001, which is lower than the .05 alpha level.

Table 11.2 Tables output for a two-way chi-square

Table of CHOICE (row) by STATUS (columns)
Frequencies

	1.000	2.000	3.000	TOTAL
1.000	20	19	3	42
2.000	6	14	5	25
3.000	2	5	10	17
4.000	6	5	5	16
Total	34	43	23	100

Test statistic	Value	DF	Prob
Pearson chi-square	22.480	6	.001
Likelihood ratio chi-square	21.993	6	.001

Coefficient	Value	Asymptotic std error
Phi	.4741	
Cramer V	.3353	
Contingency	.4284	
Goodman-Kruskal gamma	.3951	.11841
Kendall tau-B	.2790	.08642
Stuart tau-C	.2829	.08797
Spearman rho	.3097	.09626
Somers D (column dependent)	.2669	.08404
Lambda (column dependent)	.1228	.13247
Uncertainty (column dependent)	.1030	.04125

6. Write a summary statement.

For this problem, the researcher might report: "There is a significant relationship between the type of military service recruits volunteer for and their social status (χ^2 = 22.48, df = 6, p = .001)."

Other Measures of Association

In Table 11.2 other measures of association are reported in addition to the Pearson and likelihood chi-squares. The Pearson chi-square indicates whether the variables are associated; these other measures of association indicate the strength of the association. While a complete description of each measure of association is beyond the scope of this book, a brief summary follows.

Phi, Cramer V, and the contingency coefficient all quantify the degree of association tested by the Pearson chi-square. Indeed, their formulas are all based directly on the chi-square formula. For 2 x 2 tables (tables with 2 groups on both variables), phi is identical to a Pearson correlation calculated on binary variables and has values between −1.0 and +1.0 (see chapter 9). When phi is calculated for tables larger than 2 x 2, it doesn't have an upper limit and is quite difficult to interpret.

Cramer V is a slight modification of phi. Cramer V can take values from 0 to +1. A large value for Cramer V signifies that a high association exists between the variables.

The contingency coefficient is also derived from the chi-square value. Its values range from zero to some upper limit. The upper limit of the contingency coefficient depends upon the table size, so contingency coefficients should only be compared between tables of the same size. The larger the contingency coefficient, the stronger the relationship between the variables.

Goodman-Kruskal *gamma*, Kendall *tau*-B, Stuart *tau*-C, Somers D, and Spearman *rho* are appropriate when both categorical variables are ranks. Spearman *rho* (or rank-order correlation) was discussed in chapter 9. *Tau*-B, *tau*-C, *gamma*, and Somers D all use information about the ordering of the variables by considering every pair of values in the data set. The first four measures primarily differ from one another in how ties in the rankings are treated. Because Spearman's *rho* is so well known, it is the usual measure of association reported when the variables are ranks.

Lambda and the uncertainty coefficient are measures of association when the variables are measured at the categorical level. *Lambda* measures the percent of improvement in your ability to predict the value of the dependent variable once you know the value of the independent variable. Obviously, there could be two *lambdas* calculated depending on which of the two variables is considered the dependent variable. MYSTAT always calculates *lambda* using the column variable as the dependent variable.

The uncertainty coefficient is similar to the *lambda* coefficient. It measures the proportion by which uncertainty is reduced in the dependent variable once you know the value of the independent variable. Both *lambdas* and the uncertainty coefficients have values that range from zero (no improvement) to one when perfect predictions are possible.

Options in the *Tables* Dialog Box

The default values reported using the **Tables** command are the observed frequencies for each group. All the available options are in the lower-right corner of the **Tables** dialog box, which is reproduced in Figure 11.6.

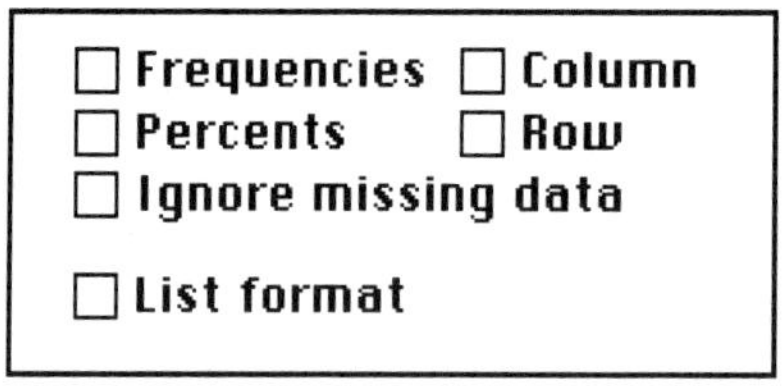

Figure 11.6
Tables dialog box options

If you click in the **Frequencies** option, MYSTAT will provide the frequencies for each cell in the table. The **Percents** option produces percentages of the total count in each cell. The **Column** option produces column percentages in each cell, and the **Row** option produces row percentages for each cell. You may choose multiple options to produce multiple tables in the same output. The **List format** option is reproduced in Table 11.3. If this option is chosen, neither the chi-square statistics nor the measures of association are calculated.

Count	CUM Count	Pct	CUM Pct	STATUS	CHOICE
20	20	20.0	20.0	1.000	1.000
19	39	19.0	39.0	2.000	1.000
3	42	3.0	42.0	3.000	1.000
6	48	6.0	48.0	1.000	2.000
14	62	14.0	62.0	2.000	2.000
5	67	5.0	67.0	3.000	2.000
2	69	2.0	69.0	1.000	3.000
5	74	5.0	74.0	2.000	3.000
10	84	10.0	84.0	3.000	3.000
6	90	6.0	90.0	1.000	4.000
5	95	5.0	95.0	2.000	4.000
5	100	5.0	100.0	3.000	4.000

Table 11.3
The **List format** option output

Other Nonparametrics

You will find other nonparametric statistics available through MYSTAT through the **Npars** command under the **Analyze** menu. These nonparametric statistics are the Sign test, the Wilcoxon signed-rank test, and the Friedman nonparametric analysis of variance. All three tests are used with dependent (correlated) samples. The Sign test and the Wilcoxon signed-rank test are both nonparametric equivalents of the dependent t-test (see chapter 6). If there are more than two dependent samples or you wish to test the same subject under more than two conditions, use the Friedman analysis of variance test (see Figure 11.1).

Sign Test

The Sign test is performed on a set of difference scores when only the sign of the differences is retained to compute the statistic. You obtain either positive or negative differences, and the number of positive differences and the number of negative differences are summed. The Sign test tests the significance of the difference between these two numbers.

The Problem The Sunfish sailing class association conducts one-design races across the world. In one-design races a person should be able to take a boat directly out of the box, rig it, and win with it. Over the years, competitors have made many modifications to their Sunfishes. One that appears to have made a distinct difference is a modification to the wooden daggerboard. Racers have strengthened the daggerboard by adding fiberglass to the outside. This increased area of the daggerboard prevents the boat from slipping sideways through the water and allows it to sail better upwind. No sailor can win a competition with a boat directly from the manufacturer. The winners are often not the best sailors but the best at laying up fiberglass.

The class association wants to market a new fiberglass board and make it the only daggerboard (no modifications) acceptable for racing. They know that the class will not accept the new board unless it is better than the old board. Eighty sailors who attend the North American Championship regatta are paired using their overall positions during the five-day event to produce 40 matched pairs. One person in each pair is randomly provided the new fiberglass board, while the partner uses the wooden board. If times were kept in the races (a continuous variable), they would not be comparable because of different wind conditions in the races. However, it is easy to determine which member of a pair wins and which loses (a binary variable). If significantly more people win with the new board, the board will have increased their speed. Since the pairs are matched on sailing performance and the boards are randomly assigned, you would expect that an equal number of winners would have wooden and fiberglass daggerboards if the board didn't affect boat speed.

The Solution

1. State the null and alternative hypotheses.

Often you see the Sign test's null and alternative hypotheses stated without symbols. You might see the null and alternative hypotheses written as follows:

H_0: There is no difference in the daggerboards.

H_1: The fiberglass daggerboard is better than the wood daggerboard.

Because the Sign test deals only with the signs of the differences (either positive or negative), another way of expressing the null hypothesis is to say that the Sign of any difference is just as likely to be positive as it is to be negative.

2. Set the alpha level.

We'll set the alpha level to .05 and MYSTAT will calculate the Sign test's value and it's probability.

3. Collect the data.

The data for this problem are found in the file *Sunfish*. When you open the data set, note that there are two variables. The first variable is WOOD: if the wood daggerboard won, a 1 is recorded; if the wood daggerboard came in second, a 2 is recorded. The second variable FIBER measures the position of the boat with the fiberglass board.

4. Calculate the statistic.

1. Select the **Npars** command under the **Analyze** menu.

    You will see the dialog box shown in Figure 11.7.

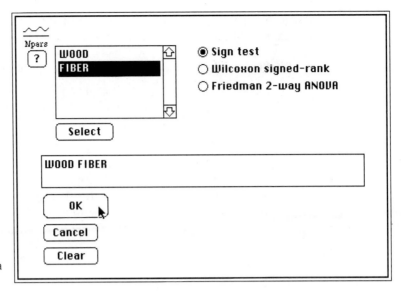

Figure 11.7
The completed **Npars** dialog box for a Sign test

2. Make sure the **Sign test** option is selected.
3. Double-click on **WOOD**.
4. Double-click on **FIBER**.

   Steps 3 and 4 indicate which variables you want the Sign test to use.

4. Click **OK**.

   You will receive the output shown in Table 11.4.

Sign test results
Counts of differences (row variable greater than column)

	WOOD	FIBER
WOOD	0	30
FIBER	10	0

Two-sided probabilities for each pair of variables

	WOOD	FIBER
WOOD	1.000	
FIBER	.003	1.000

Table 11.4
Sign test results

The first table indicates how many times the row variable had a greater value than the column variable. Note that this table is titled "Counts of differences." In the first row you see that the wooden daggerboard (WOOD) had a greater value than the fiberglass board thirty times. This means that the boat with the fiberglass daggerboard beat the boat with the wooden daggerboard thirty times. The second row indicates that the boat with the wooden daggerboard beat the other boat ten times. In the second table, the two-tailed probability of this event is calculated. The *p* value is .003.

5. Decide whether or not to reject the null hypothesis.

Since this was a one-tailed test (look at H$_1$), you can divide the *p* value in half. Because .0015 is less than the alpha level, reject the the null hypothesis.

6. Write a summary statement.

For this problem, the researcher might report: "There was an improvement in finishing positions when using the fiberglass board (Sign test = 30, p < .001)."

When the number of pairs is greater than twenty-five, the null hypothesis may be tested with a *z*-statistic. The formula for the *z*-statistic in this case is

$$z = \frac{(x \pm .5) - \frac{1}{2}n}{\frac{1}{2}\sqrt{n}}.$$

Where *x* is the smaller of the two counts of differences, and *n* is the number of untied pairs. In this problem the number of fewer signs is 10, and *n* is 40. The rule for choosing either *x* + .5 or *x* − .5 is: Use *x* +.5 when *x* < .5*n*, and use *x* −.5 when *x* > .5*n*. In this case .5*n* = 20, so you will use *x* +.5. Filling in the equation gives

$$z = \frac{10.5 - 20}{3.16227766} = -3.00.$$

You can then consult the normal distribution table in your text to determine if the results are significant. Or use the ZCF function in MYSTAT (see chapter 5). If you use the ZCF function you will note that a *z* value of −3.00 has a probability of .001.

■ The Wilcoxon Matched-Pairs Signed Ranks Test

The Wilcoxon matched-pairs signed ranks test, or Wilcoxon for short, is very similar to the Sign test. Because more information is contained in ranked dependent variables than the binary dependent variable of the Sign test, the Wilcoxon is a more powerful test than the Sign test.

The Problem The Sunfish data used for the Sign test would take a long time to produce. Each matched pair of sailors races and the winner and loser are recorded. In effect, you run forty matched races. But if all the boats could be started at one time and their finishing positions are noted, then the data is a natural for the Wilcoxon procedure because the dependent variable is of rank order. Eighty boats on a starting line would be too many, however, so only the first 20 matched pairs (40 boats) are selected to participate in this experiment.

The Solution

Steps 1–2 are identical to those in the Sign test and are not repeated here.

3. Collect the data.

The 20 matched pairs start the race simultaneously, and the race committee notes the position of each boat as it crosses the finish line. The data are contained in the *Sunfish II* file.

4. Calculate the statistic.

1. Choose the **Npars** command under the **Analyze** menu.
2. Select the **Wilcoxon signed-rank** option.
3. Double-click on **WOOD**.
4. Double-click on **FIBER**.
5. Click **OK**.

The results are presented in Table 11.5.

Wilcoxon signed ranks test results
Counts of differences (row variable greater than column)

	WOOD	FIBER
WOOD	0	12
FIBER	8	0

Two-sided probabilities using normal approximation

	WOOD	FIBER
WOOD	1.000	
FIBER	.073	1.000

Table 11.5 Wilcoxon results

The boat with the fiberglass daggerboard beat the matched boat with the wood on daggerboard twelve times, while the boat with the wooden daggerboard beat its matched pair eight times. Note that with this data set the two-tailed probabilities are .073. This is all the information you need to make your decision. For this one-tailed example, you would divide the .073 in half giving a *p* value of .0365.

5. Decide whether or not to reject the null hypothesis.

Because the *p* value of .0365 is less than the alpha value of .05, reject the null hypothesis.

6. Write a summary statement.

Because MYSTAT doesn't provide the Wilcoxon value, it can not be included in the summary statement. In this case, the following summary statement might be written: "The new fiberglass daggerboard significantly improved the performance of the racers when compared to the older wooden models (p = .0365).

■ Friedman Two-way ANOVA

The Friedman analysis of variance test is the nonparametric alternative to a repeated measures analysis of variance. It is used when you wish to compare more than two dependent samples or measures. It is often used to analyze the rankings from multiple judges.

The Problem

You are the director of research for a large marketing company. Your corporation has produced four trial versions of a new nonalcoholic beer commercial. The commercials are marketed at college-age people. You randomly select twenty college students and ask them to rank the four commercials. The dependent variable is of rank order, and because all four measures come from the same person, it is a repeated measures problem. Because there are four different measures, the Friedman two-way ANOVA is used instead of the Wilcoxon procedure.

The Solution

1. **Write the null and alternative hypotheses.**

   H_0: There are no systematic differences in the rankings across the judges.
   H_1: There are systematic differences in the ranking across the judges.

2. **Set the alpha level.**

   We'll use .05 again.

3. **Collect the data.**

   The data are provided in the *Nonalcoholic* file.

4. **Calculate the statistic.**

   1. Choose **Npars** under the **Analyze** menu.
   2. Choose the **Friedman two-way ANOVA** option.
      Since we wish to analyze all the numeric variables (AD1 through AD4), do not select any variables.
   3. Click **OK**.
      The results are shown in Table 11.6.

Friedman two-way analysis of variance results for 20 cases

Variable	Rank sum
AD1	29.0
AD2	48.0
AD3	46.0
AD4	77.0

Friedman test statistic = 35.70
Kendall coefficient of concordance = .595
Probability is 0.000 assuming chi-square distribution with 3 df

Table 11.6 Friedman two-way ANOVA results

First, each variable is listed with the sum of its ranks. Remember that each of the twenty judges ranked these four commercials. If there had been one commercial that every judge picked to be best, the sum would be 20. On the other hand, if there had been one commercial that every judge ranked last, the sum would be 80. Looking at the rank sum, note that commercial one (AD1) is close to the lowest possible score, and AD4 is close to the highest possible score. Next comes the Friedman test statistic with a value of 35.7. Following the Friedman, is the Kendall coefficient of concordance, which is an estimate of the average correlation among the judges ratings of the commercials. Finally the probability that you use to make your decision is reported.

5. **Decide whether or not to reject the null hypothesis.**

With a reported probability of .000 (which is less than .0005), you reject the null hypothesis.

6. **Write a summary statement.**

You might write the following summary statement: "The twenty judges rank ordered the four advertisements differently (Friedman test statistic = 35.7, p ≤ 0.0005). Advertisement one had the best average sum of ranks of 29. It's average ranking by the 20 subjects in this study was 1.45." The average ranking is simply calculated by taking the rank sum of 29 and dividing it by the number of judges.

■ Notched Box Plots

When working with nonparametric data, you are often interested in differences between medians rather than differences between means. Medians are better estimates of the most typical score in a distribution if the data are categorical. The notched option in the dialog box using the **Box** command under the **Graph** menu produces notched grouped box plots. When you choose this option, a notch is formed within each box at the median and the box tapers outward from this notch until it returns to its full size at the lower and upper 95% confidence intervals for the median. If the intervals around two medians do not overlap, you have 95% confidence that the two population medians are different.

182 Chapter 11 Nonparametric Statistical Tests

To have a grouped notched box plot drawn, complete the following steps:

1. Select the *Advertisement* data set.

   Referring back to the ANOVA chapter you will note that this data set consists of four different types of advertisements (GROUP) and the number of sales produced from each (SOLD).

2. Select **Box** from the **Graph** menu.

3. When the dialog box appears, double-click **SOLD** in the "Variables" box.

   SOLD is the dependent variable that will be used to construct the notched box plots.

4. Double-click **GROUP** in the "Grouping variables" box.

   GROUP is the independent variable, and MYSTAT will produce a notched box plot for each different group defined by the independent variable.

5. Make sure the **Notch** option is selected.

   The completed dialog box should look like Figure 11.8.

6. Click **OK**.

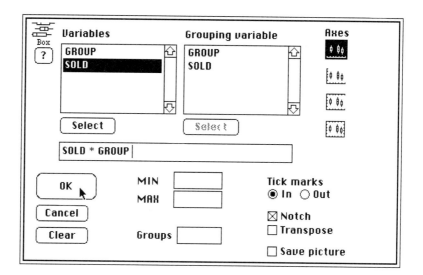

Figure 11.8 Completed **Box** plot dialog box for notched box plots

The results are shown in Figure 11.9. The median confidence intervals for groups one and two do not overlap. You are therefore assured that the medians are different in the populations represented by these two groups.

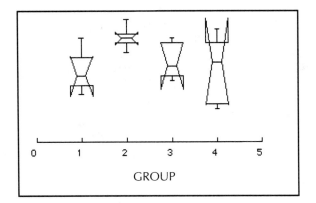

Figure 11.9
Notched box plot output for the *Advertisement* file

☞ Sometimes the confidence intervals for the medians are further out than the hinge, which makes the notched box plot fold back on itself (see the plots for groups 1, 3, and 4).

Exercises

1. A consumer-research organization asked thirty men on their college's intramural soccer team to evaluate the effectiveness of three soccer training films. After viewing each film, each man indicated the film he preferred. Using the results found in the file *Soccer*, determine whether there is a significant preference for any of the three films.

2. During the 1960s a major university wanted to know whether there was a relationship between Student's CLASS standing (freshmen = 1, sophomore = 2, junior = 3, senior = 4) and their political AFFILiation (1 = Democrat, 2 = Republican). One hundred students were surveyed and the results are tabulated in the file *University*. Were class standing and political affiliation independent using an alpha level equal to .01? Write a summary statement for this experiment.

3. During the 1960s an experiment took place to see whether a series of lectures on social awareness could influence white students in dormitories to change their attitudes about rooming with minority students. Twenty students were matched on several environmental variables that were presumed to be related to their prior exposure to minority cultures. One member of each pair was randomly assigned to the social awareness lectures and the other pair participated in a control activity. At the end of the experiment their answers to whether they were willing to live with a minority student next year were collected. Only the text output is contained in the file *Social*. You will need to use the Data Editor to change this text information into a form that can be analyzed by MYSTAT. Use the Sign test and an alpha level of .05 to evaluate these results. Did the lecture series make a difference? Write a summary statement.

4. A researcher wanted to know whether attractiveness was related to the decision to attend college after high school. The researcher collected attractiveness scores on a scale of 1 through 10 for twelve sets of male cousins, one of whom went to COLLEGE and the other who went to WORK. Use the Wilcoxon test to determine whether there is a significant difference between these cousins. Write a summary statement. The data are in the file *Attraction*.

5. Fifteen subjects were exposed to four different learning environments. The first environment gave positive rewards for correct responses. The second gave punishments for incorrect responses. The third environment terminated a loud noise when a correct response was given (negative reinforcement). The fourth environment was a control and no action was taken when the subject responded. Subjects were given the different treatments in different orders and the amount of information retained after the end of the experiment was measured. The measurement scale used is a rank order. Use the Friedman analysis of variance by ranks to evaluate the data contained in the file *Learning*. Note that the variables (ONE, TWO, THREE, FOUR) refer to the score in each of the four environments. Were there differences in the amount of information retained across the different treatments? Write a summary statement for this experiment.

6. Produce a notched box plot for the *University* data. The grouping variable is the class of the student. Hand in the plots if directed to do so. Because political affiliation only takes on two values, these plots overlap extensively.

7. Produce a notched group box plot for FSIQs in the *School Referrals* data using MDT decisions as the grouping variable. Do the same using PSYCH decisions as the grouping variable. Are there median differences between the groups? If so, which groups appear to have different population medians? You may wish to delete the case in which MDT = 7, since there is only one subject in this group. See chapter 2 for more information on this data.

References

Cleveland, W.S. 1985. *The elements of graphing data.* Monterey, CA: Wadsworth Advanced Books.

Huff, D. 1954. *How to lie with statistics.* New York: Norton.

Judd, C.M., and McClelland, G.H. 1989. *Data analysis: a model-comparison approach.* San Diego: Harcourt Brace Jovanovich.

Marascuilo, L.A., and McSweeney, M. 1977. *Nonparametric and distribution-free methods for the social sciences.* Belmont, CA: Wadsworth Publishing.

Neter, J., Wasserman, W., and Kutner, M.H. 1990. *Applied linear statistical models.* 3d ed. Homewook, IL: Irwin.

Pedhazur, E.J. 1982. *Multiple regression in behavioral research.* 2d ed. New York: Holt, Rinehart and Winston.

Siegel, S. 1956. *Nonparametric statistics for the behavioral sciences.* New York: McGraw-Hill.

Index

Symbols

(see also list on page 59)
χ^2 (chi-square), relations of frequency test 170
Y, criterion score 149
μ (*mu*), mean, means in population parameters 59
$\bar{X}$ (X bar), mean, means in sample statistics 59
r, Pearson product-moment correlation 136-141
ϕ (*phi*), phi coefficient 136
r_{pb}, point biserial correlation 136
$\hat{Y}$, predicted criterion score (expected criterion values) 149
r_s (*rho*), Spearman rank 141
s, standard deviation in sample statistics 59
σ (*sigma*), standard deviation in population parameters 59
s^2 (s-square), variances in sample statistics 59
σ^2 (*sigma* square), variances in population parameters 59
Σ (*sigma*), sum 59-60
$ (dollar sign), used following text variables 16
? (question mark), to obtain help 12
"...", (quotation marks), used around character values and spaces in text 24, 37

A

Alpha level 71
Alternative hypothesis 70
Analysis window 12, 52
Analyze menu 11
ANCOVA (analysis of covariance) 155-163
    selection criteria 156
ANOVA (analysis of variance) 99-107, 158
    command 100
    one-way 99-102
    selection criteria 98
    two-way 102-105, 180
Arrow, in scatterplot brushing 116
ASCII variable 16
Autocorrelation coefficient 146
Axes 109
Axes options 41

B

Backup disk, called data disk 20
Bars option 41
Beta weights 154
Bimodal distribution 51
Binary variables 136, 166
Bivariate regression 135, 136, 143
Box-and-whiskers plots 49-51
Box command 181
Brushing tools, in scatterplot 115
Bubble plots 127

C

Canceling a command 18, 40, 42
Capital letters differentiated from lower case 17
Character values, used in quotation marks 24
Chi-square (χ^2) test
    of independence 171
    one-way 167
    two-way 171-173
Cells 15, 17
Clear button 42
Clipboard 10, 37
Coefficient of determination 154
Coefficients, correlation 136-143, 173
Column option 174
Commands. *See individual names.*
Commands window 12
Complex find command 118, 120
Computing, using Analyze menu 11
Confidence interval 123
Contingency coefficient 173
Cook's D 150
Copy command 37
Corr command 135
Corrections 18, 62

Correlated *t*-test 85
Correlation 111
    coefficients 136-143
Covariate 156
    box 100
Cramer V 173
Criterion
    score (Y) 149
    variable 110
Critical values 71
Cursor, appearance 129
Cut command 37

D

Data disk 20
Data editor 13-38
    default display 17
    window 11, 14, 19
Data entry
    with keyboard 16
    reading in text 28
Data graphing 39-57
Data menu 11
Default
    display 17
    graph size 55
    series plots 51
Definitions. *See also symbols, commands, individual terms.*
    ANCOVA 155
    ANOVA 99
    functions 31
    operators 31
    population parameters 59
    populations 59
    relations 31
    statistics 59
    values 59
    variables 13, 59
Degrees of freedom (DF) 81, 88
Delete command (-X) 18
Deleting 18
Deletion options 140
Dependent *t*-test 85, 89-94
Dependent variables 99
Descriptive statistics 59-68
Dichotomous variables, 136

Directional hypothesis 71, 90
Distribution 60
Distribution-free tests 165
Draw line option 128
Drive button 20
Durban-Watson statistic 146

E

Editing data 18
Edit menu 10, 37
Editor menu 11, 21, 118
Error
    message 17
    Type 1 71
Error bars box 128
Errors 18, 115
Estimators, unbiased 59
Exercises 38, 56, 68, 83, 94, 105, 132, 152, 163, 183

F

Factorial designs 102
Factors
    in ANCOVA 156
    in ANOVA 99, 102
File menu 10
Fill worksheet command 32
Find commands 27, 118
Flashlight, in scatterplot brushing 117
Floppy disk installation 5-9
Font selection 36
Formats command 36
Formatting 21, 36
Formulas for calculating statistics 60
Frequencies 167
Frequencies option 174
Friedman analysis of variance test 166, 175, 180
F statistic formula 107
Further reading
    graphs 54
    nonparametrical statistics 165
    outlier detection 150

G

Gamma 174
Goodies menu 11, 54, 63

Goodman-Kruskal *gamma* 174
Goodness-of-fit test 167
Graphic design 54-56
Graph menu 11, 41
Graphs
    definition 40
    moving 54
    overlaying 129
    single-variable 39-57
Grouped data 63

H

Hard disk installation 2-4
Help (?) 12
Hinges (H), in stem-and-leaf graph 45
Histograms 40-44
Homogeneity of slopes 163
Homoscedasticity of variance 146. *See also regression line.*
Hspread 49
Hypotheses 70

I

If...then clauses 23
Independent *t*-test 85-89
Independent variables 99
Influence option 126
Influence plot 126
Initialization 3, 5
Installation of MYSTAT 2-9
Interquartile range 49

K

Kendall *tau*-B 174
Keyboard data entry 15
Kurtosis 60

L

Leptokurtic distribution 60
Leverage 149
Linear regression equation 143
Linear relationship 111
Lines for diagram, in graph dialog box 47
List format option 175

Listwise deleting option 140

M

Main effect 161
Math command 21, 74
Mathematical symbols 31
Maximum 60
MAX option 41, 128
Mean, means (μ) 59, 60, 181
Mean squares 107
Measures of association, additional 173-175
Median (M) 45 59, 181
Memory required to run MYSTAT 1
Menu. *See individual names.*
Mesokurtic distribution 60
Minimum 60
MIN option 41, 128
Mistakes, correcting 62
Modality, loss of data about 51
Mode 59
Multiple R 154
Multiple regression 135, 136
    analysis 146
MYSTAT
    button 28
    data editor 15
    definition 1
    menu bar 10, 14
    starting 9-10
    windows 11

N

Naming a file 19
Next plot command 42
Nondirectional problem 71
Nonparametric statistical tests 165-184
Notched box plots 181
Npars command 175
Null hypothesis 70
Numeric variables 16

O

OK button 42

One-sample statistical tests 69-83
    t-test 78
    z-test 75
One-way chi-square (χ^2) test 167
Open button 28
Options. *See individual names.*
Order. *See rank.*
Outlier 115, 126
    detection 149-152
Overlaying graphs 129-131
Overlay plot command 42, 129

P

Paired t-test 86, 92
Pairwise deleting option 140
Parameter 59
Paste command 37
Pearson product-moment correlation coefficient (r)
    111, 122, 136-141
Percents option 174
Phi coefficient (ϕ) 136, 173
PICT format 56
Platykurtic distribution 59
Plot
    bubble 127
    command 110
    dialog box 123, 128
Point biserial correlation (r_{pb}) 136
Pooled variance 88
Population 59
Population mean (μ) 77
Power, statistical test 156
Predicted criterion score ($\hat{Y}$) 149
Predictor variable 110
Printer selection 14
Print file 14
Print graph command 42
Printing data sets 31, 67
Print selected text command 67
Probability 71
Probability value 81
P value 107, 144

Q

Quartile 59
Quotation marks around character values 24

R

Range 59, 60
Rank 166
Rank command 35, 142
Rank-order correlation 174
Recode command 23
Redo last analysis command 63
Regress command 135, 154
Regression 135, 136
    coefficients 154
    line 122, 146
    plane 146
Relationships
    functional and statistical 114
    scatterplot 110-115
Repeated measures analysis 166
Residuals 100, 154
Resizing graphs 55
Results to command 37, 40
Rho (r) 174
Row 15, 174

S

Sample 59
Save as command 19
Save command 19
Save graph as command 56
Save picture option 56
Save residuals option 100, 145, 150
Save selected text as command 20
Saving data 19
Scale option 42
Scatter 59, 69
Scatterplot brushing 116
Scatterplots 109
    identifying data points 115
    interpretation 111
    with regression lines 122-126
    relationships 114
    two-variable 110-114
Scroll analyses box 36
Scroll bars 41
Select all command 37, 68
Select button 41
Series command 51
Series graphs 51-53

Shape. *See skew, kurtosis.*
Shift-clicking 37
Show view window 54
Sign test 166, 175-178
Six-step solution 76-78, 79, 87, 90, 93, 99, 103, 143, 147, 158, 168, 171, 176, 180
Skew 43, 60
Somers D 174
Sort command 33
Spaces in text values 37
Spearman rank correlation (r_s) 136, 141, 174
Specific cases 26
Standard deviation (S, SD, standard dev; *sigma*) 59, 60
Standard error of estimate 154
Standard error of prediction (SEPRED) 151
Standard error of the mean (Std. error, SEM) 60, 62, 77, 154
Standardize option 51
Statistical abbreviations and symbols. *See section preceding alphabetical index.*
Statistical tests
    one-sample 69-83
    selection criteria 70
    two-sample 85-95
Statistics
    descriptive 59-68
    inferential 69-83
Stats command 63
Stem-and-leaf graphs 44-48
Strength, in scatterplot relationship 112
Stuart *tau*-C 174
Studentized deleted residuals 149
Subgroups 63
Sum 60
Sum-of-squares 106
Summary statement. *See six-step solution.*
Symbol size box 127, 128
Symmetry 43, 60
SYSTAT 11
System requirements for MYSTAT 1

T

Tables command 169, 174
Tabs option 21
Tau-B 174
Tau-C 174

Tests
    ANCOVA 155-163
    ANOVA 99-107, 158
    chi-square 165-173
    correlated *t*-test 85
    dependent *t*-test 85, 89-94
    distribution-free 165
    Friedman analysis of variance 166, 180
    goodness-of-fit 167
    independent *t*-test 85-89
    nonparametric statistical 165-184
    one-sample statistical 69-83
    one-way chi-square 167
    paired *t*-test 86, 92
    power of statisticial 156
    selection criteria 70
    sign 166
    t-test 69, 78-82, 92
    two-sample statistical 85-95
    Wilcoxon signed ranks 166, 178
    z-test 69-78
Text button 28
Text files 28
Text option 21
Tick marks button 42
Tolerance values 154
Transforming data 21
Transpose box 50
T-test 69, 78-82
    selection criteria 92
Ttest command 80
Two-sample statistical tests 85-95
Two-tailed hypothesis 71
Two-way ANOVA 155-163
Type 1 error 71

U

Unbiased estimators 59

V

Values, finding 26
Variables 14
    binary 136, 166
    creating new 79, 132
    definition 59
    dichotomous 136

naming   16, 110
single, graphing   39-57
Variance   59, 60
analysis in ANCOVA   157
analysis in ANOVA   99-107
pooled   88
View window   12, 54
Visualizations. *See graphs.*

W

Weight command   35
Whiskers   49
Width option   41
Wilcoxon signed ranks test   166, 175
Windows   11. *See also individual names.*

Z

ZCF function   73
ZIF function   71
Z score   51, 73
Z-test   69-78
Z value   72

Using Software

A Guide to the Ethical and Legal Use of Software for Members of the Academic Community

Software enables us to accomplish many different tasks with computers. Unfortunately, in order to get their work done quickly and conveniently, some people justify making and using unauthorized copies of software. They may not understand the implications of their actions or the restrictions of the U.S. copyright law.

Here Are Some Relevant Facts:

1. Unauthorized copying of software is illegal. Copyright law protects software authors and publishers, just as patent law protects inventors.

2. Unauthorized copying of software by individuals can harm the entire academic community. If unauthorized copying proliferates on a campus, the institution may incur a legal liability. Also, the institution may find it more difficult to negotiate agreements that would make software more widely and less expensively available to members of the academic community.

3. Unauthorized copying of software can deprive developers of a fair return for their work, increase prices, reduce the level of future support and enhancement, and inhibit the development of new software products.

Respect for the intellectual work and property of others has traditionally been essential to the mission of colleges and universities. As members of the academic community, we value the free exchange of ideas. Just as we do not tolerate plagiarism, we do not condone the unauthorized copying of software, including programs, applications, data bases, and code.

Therefore, we offer a statement of principle about intellectual property and the legal and ethical use of software. This "code"—intended for adaptation and use by individual colleges and universities—was developed by EDUCOM. The EDUCOM code is on the last page of this book.

THE EDUCOM CODE: Software and Intellectual Rights

Respect for intellectual labor and creativity is vital to academic discourse and enterprise. This principle applies to works of all authors and publishers in all media. It encompasses respect for the right to acknowledgment, right to privacy, and right to determine the form, manner, and terms of publication and distribution.

Because electronic information is volatile and easily reproduced, respect for the work and personal expression of others is especially critical in computer environments. Violations of authorial integrity, including plagiarism, invasion of privacy, unauthorized access, and trade secret and copyright violations, may be grounds for sanctions against members of the academic community.

Questions You May Have About Using Software

a. **What do I need to know about software and the U.S. Copyright Act?**

Unless it has been placed in the public domain, software is protected by copyright law. The owner of a copyright holds exclusive right to the reproduction and distribution of his or her work. Therefore, it is illegal to duplicate or distribute software or its documentation without the permission of the copyright owner. If you have purchased your copy, however, you may make a backup for your own use in case the original is destroyed or fails to work.

b. **Can I loan software I have purchased myself?**

If your software came with a clearly visible license agreement, or if you signed a registration care, READ THE LICENSE CAREFULLY before you use the software. Some licenses may restrict use to a specific computer. Copyright law does not permit you to run your software on two or more computers simultaneously unless the license agreement specifically allows it. It may, however, be legal to loan your software to a friend temporarily as long as you do not keep a copy.

c. **If software is not copy-protected, do I have the right to copy it?**

Lack of copy-protection does NOT constitute permission to copy software in order to share or sell it. "Non-copy-protected" software enables you to protect your investment by making a backup copy. In offering non-copy-protected software to you, the developer or publisher has demonstrated significant trust in your integrity.

d. **May I copy software that is available through facilities on my campus so that I can use it more conveniently in my own room?**

Software acquired by colleges and universities is usually licensed. The licenses restrict how and where the software may be legally used by members of the community. This applies to software installed on hard disks in microcomputer clusters, software distributed on disks by a campus lending library, and software available on a campus mainframe or network. Some institutional licenses permit copying of certain purposes. Consult your campus authorities if you are unsure about the use of a particular software product.

e. **Isn't it legally "fair use" to copy software if the purpose in sharing it is purely educational?**

No. It is illegal for a faculty member or student to copy software for distribution among the members of a class, without permission of the author or publisher.

Restrictions on the use of software are far from uniform. You should check carefully each piece of software and the accompanying documentation yourself. In general, you do not have the right to:

1. receive and use unauthorized copies of software, or

2. make unauthorized copies of software for others.

This information is from a copyrighted brochure by EDUCOM, a non-profit consortium of over 600 colleges and universities committed to the use and management of information technology in higher education, and ADAPSO, the computer software and services industry association.

EDUCOM
EUIT
1112 16th St., NW
Suite 600
Washington, DC 20036

ADAPSO
1616 N. Fort Myer Drive
Suite 1300
Arlington, VA 22209-9998